Good Moms DO Cry

Good Moms DO Cry

Raising Resilient Kids
As an Immigrant Parent

LUCY CHEN

GIFTED BOOKS

Good Moms DO Cry

ISBN
978-1-966261-06-3   Paperback
978-1-966261-05-6   EBook

*To my children, who made me cry and grow.
And to my husband, who kept me
laughing anyway.*

Contents

Introduction

"Did your daughter run away from home?" My friend and colleague whispered to me in the lunch room.

"No," I answered, looking straight into her eyes.

"Is she doing drugs? Is she pregnant?" She looked worried.

"No," I shook my head many times.

"Is she trying to kill herself?" She scanned my face carefully.

Tears were beginning to fall on my cheeks.

"Gosh, no, never!" I raised my voice a little bit before lowering it. People were beginning to stare.

I thought her questions were a bit over the top; little did I realize they were far less absurd than I imagined!

"Relax, Lucy. It's fine." She handed me a box of tissues.

My friend, who was five years older than me and had emigrated from Malaysia, had a daughter who was five years older than my oldest. Not surprisingly, we had many shared interests and concerns, especially when it came to parenting. And especially when it came to raising our "rebellious" daughters.

Suddenly, the turbulent thirteens seemed as bad as the terrible twos!

When I get emotional, my tears gush uncontrollably. I feel embarrassed, like I'm regressing into a little girl. Aren't big girls not supposed to cry, as that famous Four Seasons song goes?

But of course, big girls cry. And so do good moms. As a mother of three children, I've cried many times. When I see them suffer, I cry. When they hurt my feelings, I cry. And when they wipe away my tears, I cry even more.

The simple fact is that good moms cry because we love our children. We want the best for them. Crying does not make us less; rather, it makes us fully human.

I wrote this book to help immigrant parents who feel frustrated and always anxious that they're not doing enough. This includes not only moms, but also dads.

Parenting is a journey, and life is too, so why not relax a little and enjoy the ride while we can, twists and turns included? Why see it as a chore rather than an exciting challenge?

I was glad my friend was somewhat ahead of me in the parenting journey and thus able to provide many valuable suggestions. Today, I am grateful for the many friends who listened to my worries, prayed for our family, and supported me through difficult times.

As a coach, I have also mentored and guided many young people and parents through their turmoil. Now, it's my turn to show you some lessons that I've learned over the decades, from my personal and my friends' experiences to the latest books on parenting. To protect their privacy, I've used fictional names.

If you are at the beginning of your parenting journey, this book will help you understand that more difficult and trying moments lie ahead of you. And that it's to be expected. I will show you how to cope and find more confidence in becoming the parent you want to be. These moments can include the exasperation of trying to connect with a brooding and angry teenager, the anxious feeling of being judged or compared to other parents, along with worries about your child's future, and so much more.

If you are in the middle of the journey, this book is also for you. I will show you how to become a stronger and more resilient parent so you can raise a healthier teen, mentally, emotionally, and physically.

If you are at the end of the journey, meaning that your children have already matured into strong and secure young adults, congratulations! You can relax and feel entertained while reading this book. Maybe you can even appreciate or applaud yourself for the parenting skills you've mastered on that long and sometimes unpredictable path. Laugh, reflect, and above all, celebrate.

I hope this book demystifies those limiting beliefs that can destroy parent-child relationships, such as: "I should sign my child up for an SAT tutoring class this summer," "My son should become a software engineer," and "My daughter should focus on studying first." Although it is natural as parents to harbor ambitions for our children, these "shoulds" rarely help you or your child. If anything, they can be counterproductive or even backfire badly.

Parenting is not easy. In fact, if we were to receive a license in parenting the way we do for practicing law, medicine, or K-12 teaching, we would actually find fewer guarantees. Having said that, there are certain similarities. Just like any job or career, we improve our parenting skills by being willing to learn and grow. And just like learning leadership skills in the workplace, we improve our parenting skills by learning from others, reflecting on our mistakes, and actively practicing them in our daily life.

Nonetheless, the rewards are also among the most personally satisfying.

I want you to use this book as a tool to shift your mindset. Here, I will reveal some of the most effective principles and practices that will help you in your daily life.

Parenting as an immigrant mother

Since I came to the U.S. from China thirty years ago, many of my early struggles stemmed from the cultural and language barriers that immigrants commonly face. These barriers did not end entirely when I became a mother: I now needed to grapple with cultural issues as a *parent.*

That's why I decided to write this book for immigrant parents, especially those from Asian backgrounds who are navigating the tension between their traditions and customs in a new environment. It's the tension between our understanding of hardship, scarcity, and survival as immigrants—and our children's understanding of opportunity, individuality, and Western values. Many of the stories and reflections presented here are drawn from predominantly East Asian parents raising children in a foreign country. But I believe they will resonate with other immigrant parents striving to grow, connect, and lead with intention.

You see, despite the commonality of these experiences, there are very few books written specifically for immigrant parents. Few resources speak to our dual identities. We are trying to help our children thrive in America while still holding on to our heritage. After all, generational conflict is universal, and with parenting ideas shifting so quickly, other parents may find this helpful too.

But before you go any further, let me clarify a few things. This is not a conventional "how to raise a successful child or send a child to an Ivy League university" book. In fact, this book is anything but a "Tiger Mother" book, as popularized by Amy Chua in her controversial *Battle Hymn of the Tiger Mother* (Chua 2011).

A Tiger Mother refers to a strict, demanding, and high-expectation parent who pushes her children to achieve excellence in academics, music, sports, or other pursuits. The antithesis of the "Tiger Mother" is the "Bear Child", a slang term in Chinese referring to a mischievous, unruly, or spoiled child who often behaves poorly or causes trouble, especially in public.

It's often used humorously or critically to describe kids who disrupt order or lack boundaries.

I did not attend an Ivy League university, nor did any of my Bear Children. But I succeeded in finance and technology while my children attended their dream colleges. Like me, they are happy in their careers and schools.

In Chinese and other Eastern cultures, children are part of parents' lives forever, no matter their age. This is quite different from the West, where once the child turns eighteen, the child becomes an adult and makes their own decisions. Western parents will pay children for their work while children take care of their own finances and split the bills going out. (Well, mostly.)

There are advantages and disadvantages of Eastern parenting. Advantages include the benefits of caring for each other forever. Parents tend not only to watch over their children, but also to care for their grandchildren.

Disadvantages, on the other hand, may include perennial conflict. Sometimes, children may wind up depending on their parents for every major decision while parents may harbor unrealistic expectations, wanting their children to become outstanding figures in society in order to glorify their family - so called 光宗耀祖. Even though we have mostly abandoned this outdated mindset, parents still subconsciously want their children to bring reputation and fame to the family. These sometimes unrealistic expectations can cause friction between children and their parents. At other times, cultural differences between East and West can be irreconcilable when the child decides to reject their heritage.

I am not here to judge which culture is better. However, we need to recognize that different cultures have different definitions of success, which can shape generational relationships, and by extension, parenting styles and the child's outcome.

Besides the well-known "tiger parenting" approach, which reflects authoritarian parenting, there are many other types of parenting. In the 1960s, psychologists identified four parenting styles (Lickona 2020), derived from the ideas of Diana Baumrind, a UC Berkeley professor of clinical and developmental psychology.

- **Authoritarian:** High demands, low responsiveness. Parents expect obedience and enforce rules without much explanation or warmth. While children may comply, they often struggle with self-regulation, independence and emotional well-being.
- **Authoritative:** Warm but firm. Parents set clear expectations, enforce boundaries, yet listen, explain, and support their child's autonomy. This style is consistently linked with positive outcomes, including higher academic

achievement, better emotional regulation, self-confidence and resilience.

- **Neglectful** (disengaged): Low demands and low responsiveness. Parents are emotionally distant or minimally involved and children may largely raise themselves. This style is linked with the poorest outcomes, especially in domains of behaviour, academic performance and resilience.
- **Permissive:** Low demands, high responsiveness. Parents are nurturing and supportive, but set few boundaries or expectations. Children may enjoy the freedom, yet risk lacking self-discipline, structure and the ability to manage challenges.

While authoritarian parenting is most common among Asians, which one do you see in yourself? There's no perfect parenting style. Each child and parent is different, and what works at one stage may not at another. Children don't need perfection. They need balance: warmth and encouragement alongside guidance and discipline.

If we want our sons and daughters to become more resilient and truly successful both internally and externally, we need to shift our mindset first and help them grow more freely and confidently in order for them to own their space. This book is for moms and dads who care as much about their children's wellbeing and happiness as their worldly success. It's also for those who are searching for ways to raise self-motivated and resilient kids, build stronger parent-child relationships, and most importantly, rediscover joy in the journey of parenting.

Let's begin by looking at some of the struggles that a lot of parents face today.

PART 1

WHO'S STUBBORN (ISSUES)

Chapter 1

Lose-Lose

Today, many Asian immigrant parents view their American-born and -raised children as lazy, weak, stubborn, or entitled. On the flip side, these same children tend to view their parents as overly demanding or controlling, especially in comparison with non-Asian parents. It is little wonder that parent-child conflict can be even more fraught than in other families, especially Western ones, where the conflict is usually only generational.

However, the truth is that most parents love their children and try their best to raise them while sacrificing their own interests and wants. At the same time, most children love their parents, trying their best to meet their expectations.

So what is driving this mistrust, misunderstanding, and miscommunication between parents and children?

Let's look at some factors contributing to the lose-lose situation.

Generational and Language Barriers

There's no doubt that generational tension is universal across all cultures, and this is particularly true during the adolescent years. Older generations often hope to pass down their values, guide their children, and protect them every step of the way, following the path established by their own parents. They tend to be more cautious and conservative as well, hoping that their children will avoid the mistakes they once made. On the other hand, younger generations often choose to act more openly, freely, and creatively, embracing new ideas while longing to flutter their wings and determine their own paths. These clashes have existed for centuries where tradition clashes against transformation.

Beyond generational barriers, immigrant families face an additional layer of challenge, with language playing an important role in creating conflict. Parents whose first language is not English may struggle to express themselves, while children may not fully understand their parents' deeper meaning. Children who are born and raised in America often become considerably more fluent in English than in their ancestral language, which limits deeper communication and emotional nuance between generations.

High Expectations

Some time ago, a friend from China told me that if his son ended up at a state or community college, he would carry that guilt for the rest of his life. In his eyes, attending a less prestigious school meant his son's future would be "ruined" and as a father, it would reflect his own failure to set high expectations or push hard enough. I pointed out that many American parents are proud of their children regardless of whether they attend an Ivy League or a local college, and that many of us didn't go to elite schools ourselves but still built successful lives. He quickly dismissed it: "They're Americans. For us, the whole reason we came to this country was so our children could be better off."

This reveals four important truths:

1. Immigrant families, especially Asian ones, often place extremely high expectations on their children.
2. For Asian families, education is seen not just as a value, but as a moral duty and family legacy.
3. College, especially prestigious ones, is viewed as a safety net or a key to long-term security in a foreign land, such as America.
4. As a minority in the U.S., Asians often feel insecure due to stereotypes, discrimination, or biases.

There's no doubt that expecting success can be a good thing. But when expectations become rigid and relentless, they can turn into a heavy burden for children and have a negative impact on family dynamics. The pressure on the younger generation becomes even worse when it's tied to comparison. There's a popular term called "别人家的孩子" in China, which means "other people's kids." For example, when you see your neighbor's son Tom get admitted to Harvard, or your friend's daughter Julie winning the national science bowl, you will sigh and comment with envy that they are "other people's kids," indicating that they seem to be doing better than your own.

Hustle Culture and Immigration Pressure

One common theme among people nowadays is that they are too busy. Most people are busy making money to raise a family. Some parents take on two or three jobs, which is not uncommon for those in the San Francisco Bay Area or New York, where living expenses are higher.

One YouTube video I recently watched showed a parent calculating the monthly expenditures of his family. He estimated $3,500 in rent for his family of four—including himself, his wife, and their two children, ages 4 and 8—plus at least $1,000 for groceries, $1,000 for health and car insurance, $1,000 in car loans, and $2,500 for day care and after-school care. In short, his minimum monthly expenses came to about $9,000. If they wanted to eat out, indulge in some entertainment, or save for their children's college funds, they would need a larger salary. That's about $110k annual income after taxes. This is fine if both parents work with a double income of $110K. But, if one spouse has health issues and cannot work full time, there will be serious financial strain. Such are American realities today, particularly with inflation.

This helps explain why some parents are too busy to care adequately for their children. Even some upper-income parents find themselves working overtime to maintain stability or move up the corporate ladder.

One of my friends used to fly to a different city on a weekly basis to meet clients every week. She had no time to make dinner, shop for her children, or attend their school choir performances. She felt guilty, but with a demanding job, she had no choice but to prioritize her job. Only when she found an alarming health issue did she realize she had to make major changes in her life. She realized that she had little patience with her children due to her time constraints. And not surprisingly, as an executive, she also expected a great deal from her children, wanting them to be high achievers like her.

This kind of pressure can be found in any American family but is even more pronounced among immigrant families. In order to survive, immigrant families tend to accommodate more hectic working arrangements. One of my Chinese friends, a hard-working nurse, used to work night shifts to earn the higher pay mandated by law. On top of that, she also took a second job to better support her family financially. She said this is not uncommon among her Asian colleagues. In fact, many Asian parents believe a heavy workload is necessary for raising their families and children. These parents thus rely on their extended family for support, such as grandparents, uncles, and aunts (Ali, et al. 2022). While that seems easier for the parents, it also causes issues such as lack of time with children, or mixed parenting messages when parents and grandparents use very different ways of disciplining or showing love. This is one of the factors behind strained family relationships.

Growing Pains

When we discuss the tensions between parents and children during adolescent years, we cannot forget biological causes like brain development.

According to "The Teen Brain: 7 Things to Know" published by National Institute of Mental Health, the brain is still growing during adolescence, particularly in the region referred to as the prefrontal cortex, which is responsible for decision-making, impulse control, and reasoning. Because this region does not fully develop until the mid-to-late 20s, this underdeveloped prefrontal cortex leads to conflicts between parents and children (National Institute of Mental Health 2025). Thus, it is all too easy for the teen to interpret the parent's request to clean their room as a personal attack and start launching defensive arguments.

During the earliest stage of their lives, most younger children regard their parents as God-like figures, regardless of culture. However, this perception begins to change a year or so before adolescence. They quickly realize that their parents do not know everything, especially trendy internet memes, popular music, computer games, or fashion. Suddenly, their parents appear ignorant, narrow-minded, and overly controlling.

Because children long at some level for understanding, support, and a sense of belonging among their peers at this stage in their development, they are apt to be more influenced by their friends in school than their parents. Moreover, while spending more time with their peers and less time with their families, these peer interactions are also increasingly unsupervised by adults according to Jennifer Landsford, a research professor in adolescent development at Duke University (Lansford 2025). At least, this is what studies have found when children are surveyed about who they prefer to consult for solutions.

But what about self-image and self-identity? Scientists have discovered that self-image determines success with students making significant progress when they are told they excel at math. Again, because adolescent brains have not fully evolved, teenagers not only tend to trust what others tell them, but they can become distracted or discouraged when receiving criticism. Moreover, when they spend a considerable amount of time with their friends in school, they can be more easily influenced by them, not to mention the films, TV shows, and other media they collectively watch. If they notice how their friends' parents or those they watch on TV are more relaxed about grades, they can't help but think there is something profoundly wrong with their own parents.

Similarly, when children are scolded by their parents for mistakes or misbehaviors, they can feel even more distanced and resentful. They will often claim that their friends understand them better than their parents can. So when their relationship with their friends goes south, some will feel particularly isolated and even depressed, if not suicidal in the worst cases.

Let's not forget either that since Asian-American children absorb Western values not only through their peers but their media (whether through textbooks or popular online articles) which tend to emphasize open-mindedness and support, they can also find themselves rejecting Asian mores, which lean more authoritarian. Resentment can grow when parents complain about their kids' friends who smoke, use drugs, or skip school, or when they judge their children for befriending kids of other races. Some Asian immigrant parents hold biased views, and those attitudes can create even more tension.

Asian Stereotypes and Self-image

Asian Americans, especially younger ones, face the constant pressure of both positive and negative Asian stereotypes, which adds another layer of stress. The model minority stereotype, one that was introduced in the 1960s but did not take off until the early 1980s, has proven to be limiting, even if superficially positive. It is strongly linked to the stereotype of the nerdy and bespectacled Asian male, good at academics but awkward in every other respect. Indeed, a recent analysis of films over the past 25 years published by Research in Human Development has shown that popular media has tended to portray the Asian American male as emasculated and timid (Besana, et al. 2020). On the flip side is the stereotype of the Asian female, frequently imagined as a passive and submissive lotus blossom, a view filtered through works such as *Madame Butterfly, Miss Saigon,* and *Memoirs of a Geisha.*

These stereotypes and cultural differences create additional pressure for children who wish to please their parents but also want to blend in with their peers, both white and Black. For just as parents have their own expectations that are frequently guided by their native cultural and ancestral traditions, their children are in turn guided by the cultural traditions of their classmates, teachers, neighbors, and others in their general environment, whether it be on the East Coast, Midwest, Plains or West Coast. In other words, unlike their American peers, Asian-American children not only face a generational gap but a cultural one as well. It is up to the parent, the mature adult, to navigate these waters: to understand when to be firm and when to let go.

Cultural and Technological Barriers

If parents tend to be preoccupied with providing for their families, their children generally have different concerns shaped by contemporary Western culture as seen in movies, TV, and of course, the internet. Too many of us are already aware of how teens spend an inordinate number of hours on their devices learning, communicating, and enjoying themselves. A study published in 2025 by the CDC shows that over one-half (50.4%) of teenagers ages 12-17 had 4 hours or more of daily screen time (Zablotsky, et al. 2024).

Social media and digital devices play a critical role in parent-child relationships, often creating more distance than connection. Although each generation grows up with new gadgets unfamiliar to them, the gap can feel even wider today given the speed and breadth of change; moreover, because teens can be more exposed to technology, cultural and generational conflicts can be exacerbated.

Teens can become overly obsessed with the virtual world as sports, fashion, and entertainment news occupy their attention, providing the dopamine craved by their brains, which can in turn weaken impulse control while increasing screen addiction, according to Kathryn Lorenz, MD. (Premier Health 2023).

These cultural differences between a more traditional Asian ethos that privileges education and frugality and a Western ethos that privileges personal indulgence and fulfillment can widen gaps between Asian parents and their American children, particularly when the latter are determined to reject and rebel against their heritage.

Materialism fostered by social media can be equally problematic as teens look to TikTok and Instagram to chase the latest trends, whether it be the latest lipstick hawked by an influencer or trendy sneakers worn by a star athlete. These can potentially lead them to crave a lavish lifestyle and overspend while finding dissatisfaction in their parents' more restrained spending.

I remember when a friend sobbed to me that her daughter stole her credit card to buy expensive clothes and shoes. She did not notice those purchases at the beginning, but eventually found out as the bills grew larger. When she confronted her daughter, the latter turned red, complaining that her family was too poor to outfit her properly and that she felt embarrassed in front of her girlfriends. My friend was already working two jobs to make ends meet, but her daughter did not seem to recognize her efforts and instead spent money carelessly on unnecessary items.

This is more than just a conflict over spending—it's a cultural clash added to a generational gap. In traditional Chinese culture, frugality is a virtue, and wasting money is "bad." To the Chinese mother, every dollar represented her labor and sacrifice. However, to the American-born daughter, money was not the issue, but rather her identity. She wanted to show her friends that she was just like them. She didn't want to be labeled the "poor Asian girl."

Underneath this is the rising influence of materialism, social pressure, and an ardent desire to belong. But at a deeper level, it also reflects a breakdown in communication. Many Asian parents show love through action and sacrifice, like working multiple jobs, providing food, shelter, and the best educational resources. So while Asian parents refrain from spending on themselves, they will not object to spending $100 per hour on private violin lessons for their children. At the same time, they rarely express their affection for their children through words. In Asian households, values like respect for elders, modesty, and obedience are central. Parents might scold their children when there's a conflict and expect their children to respect their authority.

In turn, an overexposure to media may lead teens to ignore their homework or other duties when they notice that (white) American parents don't pressure their kids on TV shows. This is even more the case when they see their American friends paying relatively less attention to their studies. "If Tim doesn't finish his homework, why do I need to?" They might see how these parents emphasize personal enjoyment and simple pleasures, and how they encourage success in school without forcing studying. American family vacations, birthday parties, and other activities also reflect this focus on enjoyment for children. In addition, Asian American teens may long to find the same apparent emotional affirmation and open dialogue at home too. When their own homes do not reflect Western styles, these teens may feel caught between two worlds, leading to frustration, confusion, and even resentment toward their parents.

At the same time, Asian American teens may notice either through their peers, TV, or other media, a culture that emphasizes self-expression and individual rights. They may deride their parents' sense of practicality and choose to emulate their favorite entertainers without realizing that they do not have the talent to be the next rapper or quarterback. Indeed, this intense obsession with celebrities has already been identified by the Sedona Sky Academy as "Celebrity Worship Syndrome" (Sedona Sky Academy 2024). Or they may simply rebel for the sake of it. (Let's face it, regardless of race, American teens have long enjoyed a cultural tradition of rebellion.)

Not least concerning is the abundance of misleading news or misguided opinions in cyberspace, especially when teens view their parents as hopelessly uninformed about American culture. Even the most sophisticated and literate teens are not always capable of discerning the intent of such views or identifying the shaky arguments supporting them, whether it's dubious political and cultural commentary or uninformed health advice.

What can parents do, you wonder? Parents should address these issues by having calm and nonjudgmental conversations that help teens understand the harm of some online content. Also, parents need to set clear and age-appropriate boundaries while guiding their children using digital tools in a safe manner.

But of course, parents need to model proper examples as well. Try to refrain from playing games or watching YouTube channels nonstop or scrolling through your phone in the presence of your children, actions which could give the impression you don't care about them. One can only wonder about the children of such parents. The most notorious case involves an Arizona father who left his 2-year-old daughter in a hot car while he was playing his game inside the house, leading to her death (NDTV News Desk 2024). Even his other children had frequently noticed his inattention to them while gaming.

Instead, try to learn more about your children as individuals. Try to engage in meaningful and empathetic dialogue with them by asking open-ended questions, especially if you suspect they are being swayed by harmful online content.

There's a movie that my family watched together several years ago, titled *Search*, which tells of a girl who is abducted and a father who lived totally blind to her life before suddenly realizing that he barely knew her. He did not know who his daughter's best friend was, let alone the friend's phone number and address. As it turned out, his daughter lied when she told him about studying and working on a project at a friend's house; moreover, the "friend" was not his daughter's friend at all.

With none of his friends knowing her whereabouts, her father digs into her computer and account, discovering a different life that his daughter led. She held secrets, sadness, and a loneliness he hadn't seen. This was every parent's nightmare. As I watched the story unfold, I held my breath, hoping this would not happen to my family.

After searching for 37 hours, he finally finds and rescues his daughter. I realized the danger of a hidden world behind screens, where teens can do risky things without ever disclosing secrets to their parents.

Kids nowadays spend way too much time chatting online instead of with real people. It is possible to have hundreds of friends online without any of them knowing much about you, and vice-versa. Nor should we forget that the digital world isn't just distracting, but potentially harmful with bullying and scams (Drubner 2024).

These pressures only widen the gap between immigrant parents and their children. Before we can mend the relationship, we need to understand how each side sees the other. That's where we turn next.

Chapter 2

Bear Child in Tiger Mother's Eyes

"We shape our children with our thoughts; they grow into what we believe of them."
— JOHANN WOLFGANG VON GOETHE

Bear Child (熊娃) is a term that has become trendy over recent years. It's a Chinese term that refers to an unruly, misbehaving, and socially awkward child. Somewhat belittling and a bit playful, it's used by parents when their children behave unthinkingly, with little regard for consequences. A Bear Child is usually not a great student either.

The opposite of Bear Child is "Bull Child" (牛娃), a child who's outstanding, healthy, outperforms in school, and acts like a leader, but is also respectful and well-mannered. (These terms appear to be borrowed from stock market terminology, with a "bear market" suggesting a bad market and "bull market" its opposite.) Not surprisingly, parents tend to prefer such children since they also want to be credited for raising such a child.

But the reality is that traditional Chinese goals are not easy to pursue in a new land and culture.

Many Chinese immigrants like me have worked hard at school and earned advanced degrees before settling down. We raise our children with hopes that they will repeat our success, or better yet, surpass us—whether by attending a better school, building a flourishing career, becoming more successful in life, or all three. Indeed, raising an outstanding child can be said to be part of our American dream.

However, like us, our children have their own aspirations and ambitions. Their definitions of pleasure and success may diverge and this should not be surprising when we think about it. After all, they are growing up in a different culture from ours with different ideals, habits, and mores: for instance, being individualistic versus collectivist. Living more in the present than the future.

But first, let's examine some of these complaints about Bear Children.

1. **"Kids are too entitled nowadays."**

My friend Kelly called me around 9 one evening about her daughter Joan.

"Joan was like an angel, so soft, gentle, and cute when she was a baby, but now she's like a monster. She suddenly changed into a different person."

"How so?" I asked. I couldn't believe it.

"It's like she's grown spikes all over. She's irritable. She now talks back and yells at me. The other day, she even slammed the door and almost hit my head when she flung a notebook across the room. Even when I try to talk to her about dinner and offer to make her favorite food, she pretends not to hear. And sometimes, she rolls her eyes when telling me to leave her alone." Kelly sighed and coughed.

"Are you sick?" I asked.

"It's been three days, but I'm better. I'm sick, but I still try my best to cook dinner for her after work. She does not care about my health at all. She only comes to me for money for parties with her friends. It's like I'm an ATM that spits out money. I work so hard to pay the mortgage, buy clothes for her, and send her to private tutoring. I don't see any appreciation." Kelly paused, probably looking at her watch.

"I need to check on my cake in the oven. It's for the teacher's appreciation lunch tomorrow. Thanks for listening to my rant." She sighed again.

I empathized with her, knowing how deeply hurt she must have been by her daughter's disrespectful behavior.

But I knew she was not alone. I had heard many other similar stories.

2.   "Kids are too weak."

"Kids nowadays are too weak." Another friend, John, complained to me. He was referring to his daughter Eve.

"Eve organized an event at school to sell baked goods. Her friend signed up to help her, but did not show up. She had to do all the work herself. She had a fight with her friend. Maybe her friend said something mean so she quit her club President role. She cried for a couple of days." John scratched his head.

"She got a B in AP Calculus; she cried. She lost her tennis match; she cried. Her friend did not invite her to their party; she cried. She's just too weak." He shook his head.

"When I was her age, nothing could beat me. If someone criticized me, I did not care. Even though I was bad at math, I studied even harder. It became a piece of cake. Just push yourself harder. That's the solution. But she will not listen…" John wrapped up his story, clearly frustrated.

3. "Kids are too lazy."

Another complaint I often hear from my friends is that their kids are too lazy. They scatter their clothes all over the room and step over the mess without bothering to pick anything up. Their rooms are like a pigsty, full of garbage with dirty socks strewn everywhere, candy wrappers and chip bags spread from bed to desk. There are markers without caps and contents of a dirty lunchbox on the desk.

I saw an online news report mentioning an angry father who moved his daughter's furniture and belongings to the street in front of his house (Levin 2016). Although he repeatedly urged his daughter to clean her room, she ignored him. Frustrated, he had decided to expose her messiness to the world.

I felt embarrassed for his daughter, but as a parent, I understood all too well the frustration of the father. While his method may not have been the most tactful way to teach his daughter a lesson, it was nonetheless understandable.

4. "Kids are too obsessed with toys and gadgets."

For many years, one of the most devastating parental complaints about their children is digital addiction, one topped only by drug addiction.

One exasperated friend, Laurie, told me that her son Jonathan seemed to play computer games every minute outside of school. Whenever she walked into his room, he was often playing a game. Jonathan was even reluctant to eat dinner outside of his room. "He's like a sticker stuck to the computer desk and his eyes will not even move away from the screen. He's too focused on his virtual world rather than anything happening around him. To him, advancing to the next level would be the most important thing in the world."

Laurie tried to discipline him, but to no avail. She turned off the Wi-Fi by 10pm, but Jonathan figured out how to crack the password after she went to sleep. Despite using intimidation and enticement, she found him unmoveable, for he was smart enough to find a way to play. She found it depressing that her son seemed to care for computer games more than anything else, including her.

5. "Kids lie flat."

There's a trendy saying in China, "躺平", that translates to "lie flat" in English. It describes the mindset and behavior of many young people who have no motivation to work hard by either advancing their career or making money. They may have tried to study but found the outcome less than satisfactory. Tired of meaningless chasing, pushing, and trying, they decide to lie down and rest. They do the bare minimum of work to maintain independence or minimum homework to avoid failure. They enjoy lying on couches and doing nothing. At least, that's the image associated with "lie flat." Unmotivated is the word for them.

Many older people find it difficult to understand this attitude and lifestyle because they cannot understand such a lack of drive and ambition. When "those young people" happen to be their own kids, they find it even more infuriating.

"When I was young, I worked hard to get an A. I wanted an A in every subject. I wanted to win the first prize at all competitions, or at least I tried hard," a father told me.

"I studied and practiced day and night. That's why I could get a high score on the GRE and receive a full scholarship to an American university. I always pushed myself hard and I was motivated to improve myself. That's how I was able to get a graduate degree and find a job and raise a family. I just don't understand young people who want to lie flat… My son is this way. He feels good about getting a B and does not want to study hard," he continued to vent.

"We immigrant parents work so hard to reach this level. But, kids do not seem to care. Why? Do they intend to rely on us forever? " he stared at me, searching for answers.

His last sentence reveals an even worse scenario for many immigrant parents - their children never becoming independent. There's another popular word in recent years in China, "啃老", (often likened to the Western term NEET - Not in Education, Employment or Training), describing young adults who remain financially dependent on their parents well into adulthood.

I could understand his exasperation. What he described is something many immigrant parents in my circle pay close attention to and actively expect their children not to fall into.

Indeed, even though there are not many such children in my circle of friends, I have heard a few complaints from immigrant parents about their kids who stay with them and have no jobs after college. It has become the worst parental nightmare.

6. "Kids give up too easily."

"Kids nowadays give up too quickly and easily. Today's children are too squeamish to endure hardship. When someone says something, they give up. When the weather is cold, they say it's too cold and they won't practice for that day; when the weather is hot, they say it's too hot and they won't practice for the day. They have so many excuses," one friend lamented.

"When I was little, we ran one mile every day at school. That was the first thing in the morning. Sometimes it was below zero outside. Even then, we still ran on the frozen cement road. When the wind brushed my face, it was like a knife cutting into my skin. My tears were all over my face because of the cold wind. I did not like it, but I had no choice. The teacher said it was to build our bodies and characters. I believed him. Look at me and my classmates, we turned out to be tough and resilient," she nodded, looking wistful as if longing for the past.

Her daughter gave up soccer, switched to swimming, then gave up on swimming after one year.

Academically, her daughter refused to participate in the Science Olympiad club because she did not like the pressure of studying and practicing for the competition. Once again, the mother thought the daughter quickly gave up on anything hard.

7. "Kids are too stubborn."

Another challenge is that kids may seem too stubborn to follow their parents' instructions and wishes. What a difference from our childhood when we listened to parents and respected their opinions and authority! But nowadays, things are different. Whether they're in China or the US, kids are more likely to express their own opinions and be less willing to obey their parents, especially when they become teenagers. This includes minor things such as what clothes they wear and food they eat, as well as the subjects they prefer to study and careers they hope to pursue. To some parents, it feels like their kids won't turn back or listen until they hit a wall themselves—no matter how many warnings they're given. In Chinese, we call it 不撞南墙不回头, meaning one does not change course until they hit the wall before realizing the hard way.

"I suggested that my daughter write about environmental issues and global warming as the topic for the scholastic essay, but she did not want to listen to me. She wrote about mental health instead. Just as I expected, she did not win. When selecting a college major, I told her to consider computer science, but she wanted to study history. She needed to listen to me, as I have insights and experience. Computer science will make it easier to find a job. Studying history could be fun, but not for a major. Not a lot of jobs out there… It's so hard to be a parent nowadays. Kids just don't want to listen. Too stubborn," she sighed.

She's a software engineer and gets paid a high salary in Silicon Valley. Her old major was Japanese. Discovering there might not be a job after graduation in the U.S., she switched her major to computer science. Even though she had no background in programming, she pushed herself to study harder and catch up. Eventually, she got a M.S. degree and secured a job.

She hoped that her daughter would turn around when she "hit the wall" later on.

I am sure that there are plenty of other complaints from parents about their children. The list of complaints could be as long as this whole book. Basically, parents feel that their children do not live up to their expectations. Period.

But…

I'm not finished yet.

This is just the perspective from parents.

What are the opinions of their children (or Bear
Children)?

Chapter 3

Tiger Mother from Bear Child's Perspective

"Children are not things to be molded, but people to be unfolded."
— JESS LAIR

Many Asian kids grow up under the parenting of a Tiger mother who's strict, demanding, and never seems satisfied. Kids are scared to mess up, embarrassed when criticized by their moms in front of others, and annoyed when they are constantly compared to someone else's child. They feel like they are always being pushed around, told what to do, what to study, even what career to pursue.

The concept of the Tiger Mother became a phenomenon fourteen years ago when Amy Chua published her book, *Battle Hymn of the Tiger Mother.* The reactions were immediate and deeply divided. The book resonated with a number of Asian parents, partly because her stories and lessons sounded so familiar: be strict with your children, hold a high standard for them, and push them to achieve more. At the same time, some readers, including Asian parents, criticized her harsh, strident ways, even considering her cruel and abusive.

I could not condone the harsh methods she used in punishing her daughters. Yet, I knew they were not uncommon, since a few of my friends were also quite rigorous when it came to discipline and expectations. Regardless of our views as parents, we should also consider the child's perspectives. How does the Bear Child view the Tiger Mother?

1. **"Mom constantly asks me, 'Why didn't you get an A?!'"**

"A is for Asians. You've got to get an A for all subjects. That's what my mom told me," said an Asian boy.

"But, how can I get straight A's? Too much pressure. What's wrong with getting a B? My friend Tom got a B and his mom celebrated it. If I get a B, my mom gets so mad at me!" he continued.

I read this conversation online many years ago and found it both interesting and funny. I know that many Asian parents, including myself, want their child to get straight As.

"Even though I got an A, my mom asked me if there's extra credit so I can get an A+. Or, she would ask how many students got an A. It's like, it's easy and normal to get an A. Getting an A will not earn me any praise…Sometimes, she will ask if I'm number one in the class or who's the number one kid?A typical Tiger mother!" the boy added, along with a shrug emoji.

2. "No piano anymore"

Piano lessons for children are very common in Chinese-American families. Parents want to provide their sons and daughters with an opportunity to learn music, an opportunity that some lacked as children when raised with scarce resources and poor living conditions in their native countries.

When I grew up in China, my family could not afford instruments or lessons—nor could friends' families, given widespread poverty during the 1970s and '80s. My father played several musical instruments including piano, violin, and flute, and regretted not spending his meager resources to buy me one when I was young. That's why he encouraged my daughters to learn, even buying my second daughter a violin. For those of us who missed the opportunity to learn, we long for our children and grandchildren to compensate for our losses, as it were.

However, children can easily feel pressured because learning an instrument requires frequent and diligent practice. Sometimes it's not easy for younger children to sit at the piano for more than half an hour, let alone an hour a day.

Not surprisingly, struggles between children and parents have become all but normalized among my friends' families. Some children may obey while parents may compromise. One of my friends used similar methods like Amy Chua and forced her younger daughter to learn a piano composition.

"I hated it," the daughter told me. "Why did my mom push me so hard? SHE does not even know how to play piano herself! She always says it's for my own benefit, but I don't see how. It's torture. She keeps pushing me to advance to the next level, level 5, then level 6, then level 7… Never ending."

Later on, in an effort to end the family war, the mother stopped pushing the daughter. Peace returned.

Another family was not as fortunate. After many years of fighting and tears, the daughter finally achieved level 10, the highest one.

On the day she received the certificate, the daughter handed it over to her mom, saying, "There you go. Happy now? No piano anymore."

The daughter never touched the piano again.

3.   "They never listen"

"My mom nags me all the time, nonstop. Repeating the same thing over and over." When I heard this comment from a girl one day, I smiled to myself.

Isn't that the same feeling I had as a daughter? Even when I was much older, my parents still reminded me to watch traffic, drive safely, and eat more fruit in every conversation. Of course, they were reminders with good intentions. For many Asian families, this love is expressed not through hugs and words, but through constant reminders.

"She does not listen," the girl sighed.

I believed her partly because many parents are indeed unable to stop talking and listen closely to their children. Instead, parents are on a mission to pour out their experiences and advice to their children in the hopes they will avoid mistakes and live better lives.

But from the child's perspective, the constant advice and exhortations were tiresome. One time, my daughter was telling me about her struggles and frustration at school. I jumped in, trying to find a solution for her. I tried to commiserate by mentioning how my childhood was also full of tough moments and how I persevered to overcome these difficulties.

Her lips quivered as she asked me, "Mom, why is it always about you? I'm the one having trouble and needing help…"

I suddenly realized that she was right—I was always talking about my own life experiences while forgetting to listen to her story and feelings.

On another occasion, my friend told me about an argument she had with her son. She wanted her son to join the debate club, hoping he would gain communication and leadership skills. She continually reminded her son that he needed to improve in those areas. Also, it would be nice for him to win awards for his college applications. Thinking it was all for his own good, she nudged him for many days, even though he told her numerous times he was not interested in public speaking. The son covered his ears as his mother nagged him.

Finally, he jumped up, yelling, "You always criticize me. You never listen. I hate my life!"

The mother froze. She later realized that even though she thought she was delivering caring words, her words sounded like hurtful criticism to her son. For too long, she had never listened to his side of the story.

4. "I'm never good enough"

One of the common complaints from children about their parents is that their parents don't think they are sufficiently accomplished.

A friend's son complained to his mother one time, "You pushed me to sign up for the Science Bowl. After our team won in the area, you told me to win the regionals and even nationals. It seems like it will never end..."

This is a very common phenomenon among Asian immigrants since parents have high hopes for their children. After all, they rationalize, they uprooted everything to move to America, wanting their children to realize their lifelong dreams.

That's why so many Asian parents sign up their children for after-school tutorial classes, hoping the classes will help them achieve even more academically. SAT classes are a must for many Asian students, who spend their free time studying because of parental pressure. In the movie "Di Di", a 13-year old Taiwanese boy has to attend a SAT class during weekends because his mom pushes him to study, like other Asian students.

"I told my son he's my only hope. He needs to study tirelessly in order to succeed," a friend of mine shared with me one day.

"What was your son's response?" I asked.

"I don't know… He studies hard, but still not enough. When I was his age in China, I studied fourteen hours a day and did nothing else besides sleeping and eating. That's how I was accepted into a good college here and got a scholarship," the mother answered proudly.

Her son did very well at school, going so far as to be accepted at an Ivy League school. However, he told his mother he felt immense pressure growing up.

"I am never good enough for you—admit it," he told her.

His mother was speechless.

At the same time, Asian parents tend to criticize their children for their mistakes harshly, even in public.

"Don't be disrespectful to elders."

"Don't be lazy."
"Don't be a quitter."
"Don't be weak."
"Work harder."

Lia Huynh, a licensed marriage and family therapist, points out that Asian parents can be overly obsessed with their children's performance. She states, "I'm not saying that children should be enabled to be lazy and not work hard, but I think that if all a person's worth is in their performance and that's all that they are praised for, I think that can be detrimental." (Huynh 2025).

Many comments and criticisms can usually be traced back to culture and customs, where blunt statements like "you are too fat" or "don't be too proud" are made openly. These comments can be harmful to their children, especially in front of their friends. No wonder children feel that they are never good enough in their parents' eyes.

5. "They always compare"

I overheard a joke about a conversation between a father and his son.

The father said to his son, "Look at your friend Tom! He's very clean and well mannered. He studies hard and gets good grades. Why can't you be just like him?"

The boy answered, "Look at your friend Scott! He's wealthy and kind. He runs his business successfully and has become a multimillionaire. Why can't you be just like him?"

The point is that no one likes to be compared with other people, especially children. Many Asian parents tend to compare their children to other children, sometimes intentionally and at other times by accident. I used to compare my daughters with other children unconsciously.

"I heard that Amy won a scholastic art award last week. How exciting! Her painting will be displayed at a Congressional building… You keep up your good work and some day you will win the award as well." I excitedly told my daughters at the dinner table.

They did not respond immediately. I thought they did not hear me or did not care about Amy or her award. They continued discussing the new meme on the internet.

I eventually realized that my daughters heard every single word. They were happy for Amy of course, but they had to assess the expectation from the tone of my announcement. Even though I was not comparing them to Amy directly, I actually did hope that they would be just like her and win an award.

At one time, my daughter casually mentioned to me, "Lily's mom always compares her with other kids. Lily hates it so much. Why do parents always compare us?"

"I don't compare you with other kids, do I?" I looked at her.

A silent moment.

Obviously, I am one of "those parents."

In their eyes, parents are prone to comparing their children with their peers in order to stimulate progress. But their children hate comparisons, period.

6. "I cannot make my own decisions"

Many Asian children are urged to obey their parents because filial respect is part of the culture. Some families help their children make all decisions, from minor things such as clothes and food, to more significant ones such as friends, academic activities, and college majors. This is hardly surprising since Asian parents are more concerned about job security than anything else, which is why they force their children to major in engineering, accounting, medicine, or law. In some families, this decision-making influence eventually extends into romantic relationships and marriage as well.

At one party hosted by a friend from China, we discussed our children's allowance, such as how often and how much we give them.

One mother said, "I don't give my son any allowance. What if he spends on inappropriate things like drugs, cigarettes, or alcohol?"

Another mother said, "Allowance? For what? For helping me do the dishes? That's my daughter's duty. I cook dinner and it's her duty to help with the house chores."

While a lot of us nodded along, one father stood out. "My son refuses to receive money from me."

We all turned our heads looking at him, commenting, "Wow. A good son who knows it's his duty to help out."

"No, not like that. He said, 'Even if you give me money, you will not let me spend it on things like computer games and toys. Why bother to give me money if you don't want me to spend it?'" the father scratched his head, blinking his eyes.

From the son's point of view, his parents did not allow him to make decisions on his own.

Another boy in our circle wanted to major in art because of his exceptional skills in sculpture and painting. However, his parents insisted that he study computer science because of its numerous professional opportunities.

He ended up studying computer science after being pressured by his parents. Nor is he an exception, since many Asian kids wind up majoring in subjects chosen by their parents even if they are not interested. Among those who heed their parents, some may wind up feeling fulfilled while others may begrudge their parents and end up breaking off all contact with them. Even those who do wind up pursuing their interests may blame their parents for a late start, especially if it has a negative impact on their career.

Even where romantic relationships are concerned, some of my friends tell their children they must find a spouse of Asian descent, preferably of their own ethnicity in order to avoid language and cultural barriers.

In their children's eyes, freedom is a faraway concept because they cannot make their own decisions.

7. "Mom always says mental health is fake"

It's not just Asian parents who don't understand or accept the concept of mental health. For many American parents, especially pre-Gen X, it's a relatively new concept. What makes things worse is that such parents believe mental disease only boils down to a child's vulnerability, and that therefore it is shameful. On top of this, traditional Asian culture is also bogged down by shame culture, which balks at disclosing anything that might damage family reputation. The Chinese refer to it as "家丑不可外扬", meaning "do not make family scandals public."

"My daughter said it's all because of us that her treatment was delayed," a mother cried to me about her daughter.

She was a smart girl, but during her teens, she became depressed and eventually stayed at home for a year. Her mother did not take her to see a therapist until her condition worsened to the point where she did not want to go out or talk to anyone.

Believing her depression was caused by her parents, the girl blamed her parents for not treating it seriously and thereby delaying her diagnosis and treatment.

"You thought you care about me. You thought I could be healed by good food. You thought you gave me everything I needed. Mental problems are serious issues. You just cannot accept that you have a daughter who's mentally ill," the girl accused later on.

Some parents refuse to learn about mental health issues. They live in their own bubbles and do not want to open to the world outside of their house. We will discuss mental health issues further in Chapter 8, Mend the Fence.

8. "THEY don't want to learn, but they push ME hard!"

"Steve pushed Helen so hard on playing piano, studying AP Algebra, and joining the debate team. Everything. Meanwhile, he never wanted to improve *his* English," a friend of mine, Janice, smiled bitterly. Steve, her husband, often has arguments with their daughter Helen.

"She complained to me all the time, saying 'Dad is so mean,'" she continued.

"Did she make such a suggestion to her dad?" I asked curiously.

"She has, but Steve responded, 'I'm too old to learn anything. You are young and you should learn more.' So, Helen rolled her eyes at her dad. I cannot do anything about it," Janice shook her head.

Steve lived in his Chinese world—eating Chinese food, speaking Chinese, using Chinese apps, watching Chinese TV programs, and retaining a very Chinese mindset. There was nothing wrong with any of this, since it was simply in his comfort zone. The problem was that he refused to listen to his daughter and did not understand that she had adopted American ways by being raised in America. At the same time, Steve did not want to learn new things, yet pushed Helen to do exactly that. In other words, he did not set a proper example for her.

This double standard naturally created friction. Their mindsets and thought processes were different. There were fewer and fewer common topics for the dad and daughter to talk about.

"When I try to discuss sports, movies, and local news, my dad has no idea of what I am talking about. He lives in America, but he never wants to learn anything outside of his world," the girl told her mom. Stories like Steve and Helen's remind us that connection requires effort from both sides and parents must lead first.

So far, in Part 1, we've explored some of the friction between parents and children. But what can we do to resolve these issues?

Also, bear in mind that parent-child conflicts are nothing new or special and have existed between generations for centuries. So why have these conflicts flared up in recent years?

Many of the examples I've shared in this chapter reflect patterns commonly associated with an authoritarian parenting style (strict, demanding, and low on warmth). It's important to acknowledge the limitations of this approach. Children raised in such environments often internalize the belief that they are never good enough. This can erode their confidence and discourage them from trying new things and can even prevent them from becoming successful. Numerous studies show that authoritarian parenting is also strongly associated with poorer mental health, higher anxiety and depression, and lower self-esteem. Some cause greater behavioral difficulties in children and adolescents (Delvecchio, et al. 2020).

PART 2

FROM STUCK TO STRONG

Chapter 4

Principle 1: Communicate, Communicate, Communicate

"The biggest communication problem is we do not listen to understand - we listen to reply."
— STEPHEN R. COVEY

"Fine. Do whatever you want!" I slammed the door shut and stormed out.

It was one of those moments I could not restrain my anger when my daughter refused to complete her missing homework. I didn't want to see a red mark on her report card. After trying various rounds of persuasion, bribery, and firmness on her, I realized I had failed and left in defeat. How could I talk to her effectively?

It's a question that continues to dog so many parents.

When I started this book, I surveyed my friends, asking what were their main concerns about parenting. The foremost was communicating with their children.

On one hand, as parents, we often pour our hearts out, sharing the hardships we've endured and the life lessons we've learned over the decades in the hope that they will move and influence our children. Yet, they remain indifferent, appearing to turn a deaf ear.

On the other hand, our children seem to enjoy their social media feed and other not-so-good advice from their equally callow friends.

Kids nowadays have more information at their feet than ever before with the availability of the internet. It includes everything from legitimate sources of information to dubious claims on social media: they can learn how to make an egg salad as easily as learning to make an explosive device.

In short, it's not so much that we face unprecedented challenges as parents, but rather that there are so many more challenges today in the shape of plentiful, competing sources of information for our children, and they are all taking place at a greatly accelerated speed, no less.

It took me a while to realize I should not have slammed the door. But then again, my children slammed the door on me many times. I had to ask myself, did they copy me or did I copy them?

Either way, neither was good.

Shut Up and Listen (Active Listener)

When it comes to communication, we all understand the importance of active listening and tactfulness. We do it at work, talking to our bosses, discussing projects with our colleagues, and negotiating with our clients. But somehow, when we talk with our children, we tend to behave in nearly the opposite fashion, assuming the guise of a not-so-patient boss. We keep talking and repeating ourselves, forcing them to listen to us.

Not surprisingly, this frustrates them. Perhaps it's time for us to shut up and listen.

One friend, Jane, confessed her struggles to me several years ago. Her teenage daughter Joanna complained that her algebra class was much too challenging for her. Although the mother offered to tutor her daughter, the latter refused, saying she would definitely fail no matter what. Jane then offered to find a tutor, but Joanna refused that as well, saying she tried it but it did not work.

"I'm just dumb. I'm going to fail the class." Joanna burst into tears.

Jane got annoyed. What a crybaby, she thought.

"When I was little, I studied hard. If I feared I would not get an A, I would put extra time and effort into studying. Crying won't help," she could not have sounded less sympathetic.

Joanna grew angry. "Are you saying I'm not only dumb, but also too lazy to study and weak?"

Jane felt offended. "No. I'm just trying to help. Telling you the right way to get a good grade. When I was little…"

"Why do you always mention when you were little? And why do you always criticize me? You were better than me, ok? I hate myself," Joanna interrupted.

Jane almost responded with "I was not criticizing you," but suddenly realized the conversation was going nowhere.

In order to deescalate the heated conversation, Jane knew she had to stop. She returned to her own room to reflect more closely on the situation. Maybe her daughter had rightly detected a certain sense of superiority in her, namely, that she believed Joanna was not as capable.

Jane continued to reflect on her relationship with her other children. It occurred to her that she was always trying to solve problems for them, acting as the problem solver, hero, and savior. Her interruptions hindered Joanna's expression. Maybe Joanna didn't need quick solutions so much as to be heard.

The next day, after sleeping on it, Jane decided to listen to her daughter's story again, without jumping to conclusions or offering additional help.

After cooking a favorite meal for Joanna, Jane gave Joanna a big hug. When the house felt more harmonious and peaceful, Jane asked Joanna about her progress in algebra. This time, Jane patiently nodded, offering tissues, and looking at Joanna sympathetically as the latter told her more, adding details to her story. She had been assigned to work with three boys for a group project during class. Whenever she could not solve problems on the assignment, the boys would only make eye contact amongst themselves and snicker while shrugging their shoulders. At one time, she overheard them saying "girls suck at math."

Joanna felt ashamed and miserable, and worse of all, began doubting herself. Was she doomed as a girl?

After hearing Joanna's story, Jane hugged her again. She realized that Joanna only wanted a caring listener. Joanna found comfort after venting her worries and struggles.

My friend later on shared that she was almost tempted to put on her Wonder Woman cape to rescue her daughter. But fortunately, she restrained herself. As it was, Joanna found her own solution. She asked her teacher to reassign her to another group of students she felt comfortable with. She got an A at the end of the semester.

What did the mother learn? She learned that it was better to be a cheerleader than a nagger.

Use Courtesy, not Curtness

"Time to get up! You are going to be late for school!"

"Your room is too messy. Clean it up!"

"Do your homework now! Don't play computer games."

"Put down your phone when we're eating dinner."

"Stop whining. Just finish it."

Are these phrases familiar? Parents complain, yell, hush, and push, but their kids don't respond.

One friend expressed some degree of shock when she told me about how her daughter responded after being advised to clean her room. "Why do you always criticize me, Mom?"

My friend's intention was actually to offer help, but her daughter interpreted her gesture as criticism.

One important lesson in communication I learned at work over the years is to ask questions - not just any questions, but open-ended questions. Bear in mind that being a parent is not unlike being a manager who motivates team members: in both cases, we want others to listen and follow.

Open-ended questions provide three important benefits.
1. Engage in a real conversation instead of criticizing.
2. Hear your child's side of the story before jumping to a conclusion too quickly.
3. Give some control to your child instead of acting as a problem solver.

Think about the commands at the beginning of the section. Reframe them into questions like:

"What can you do to help yourself get to school a little earlier in the morning?"

"How would you like to neaten your room?"

"How long do you plan to play computer games?"

"How would you feel if everyone looked at their own phone on the dinner table?"

"What's your plan to get things done?"

Open-ended questions usually start with "when", "what", "who", and "how". Avoid "why," which may sound like you're criticizing them—for instance, "Why is your room so messy? Why can't you do your homework first before playing computer games?"

In a challenging situation, children benefit from a coach, not a savior. As their coach, we help our children cultivate a healthy independence. Our open-ended questions can help them examine each option more closely. At the same time, these questions should be neutral, avoiding overtones of criticism or condemnation. Our task is to allow them to think deeply about the possible choices and the final decision lies in their hands.

In addition, they might not even need our help. They may only need someone to listen to their issues and concerns. Overall, open-ended questions provide greater support, revealing our understanding and love.

For example, one friend June spoke to me about her college daughter Samantha's roommate problems. The roommate used her printer and paper several times without telling her.

"When I needed to print my project, I found out we ran out of paper yesterday. How could she do that to me? So inconsiderate. I did not sleep well last night," Samantha complained.

June listened patiently to Samantha before saying, "It must be hard for you. What are you going to do?"

Samantha sighed, "I don't know."

June felt an urge to say "Talk to her again and give her an ultimatum," "Find another roommate," or "Just hang on there for another two months till the end of the semester." But June held her tongue.

Instead, she asked Samantha, "What's the best way to solve it?"

Samantha paused and said, "I have mentioned it to her a couple of times, but she always said she forgot. Maybe I'll put a sign on top of the printer."

June nodded, "Ok, what if it doesn't work?"

Samantha thought about it and replied, "Thank you for listening to me."

June concluded to me that Samantha did not want solutions from her, but rather, emotional support. Her open-ended questions wound up providing a safe space.

Honey, Honey, Honey (Praise)

People cherish compliments and terms of endearment because they reaffirm one's values while boosting self-image. When our children are young, we typically use terms of endearment like "precious," "honey bun," and "sweetie," even when not praising them.

When they grow older, however, we tend to avoid such words altogether. Moreover, Chinese culture tends to discourage frequent praise after a child has passed the age of ten; this is particularly true for boys who are raised to be "tough." "Honey, honey, honey" is only for girls.

But we should never forget that words of approval can easily light up someone's day. Think about the times when the boss or a coworker expresses appreciation for our work. At home, family members can use words of appreciation as well.

Whenever my father complimented me for keeping my room tidy, I felt so proud of myself. I would show him again the next week and the week after.

In her book *Mindset: The New Psychology of Success,* Dr. Carol Dweck emphasizes the importance of praising effort, persistence, and strategy, which fosters motivation and resilience. She warns that praising intelligence can backfire and undermine confidence and performance (Dweck 2007), since complimenting a child's given gifts may shift the focus away from effort. In other words, when your child gets an A, you should praise them for hard work rather than native smarts.

However, I recommend we praise our children for both. When we see an infant, we naturally marvel at their chubby face, lovely hair, and soft skin. "What a cutie! Such an angel!" These praises come out of our mouths naturally as our acclamation lights up the room for both the mother and baby. We can still praise older children not only for their looks and intelligence because these are God-given traits, but also for other characteristics such as grit, kindness, and optimism.

Praise can transform misbehaving children into polite and disciplined students by helping them gain confidence, regard themselves in a more promising light, and believe that anything is possible with solid effort. After all, we've all heard stories about students who've managed to improve their failing grades tremendously after switching to a more encouraging teacher.

Praise is also an effective way to connect with others. Here, I'm referring to sincere praise, not false or disingenuous praise. We parents need to compliment our children more often, even when we personally don't think they deserve it altogether. That means telling them about their good traits but holding up room for improvement in other areas. When I coach clients on parenting, I always suggest they praise their children at least once a day. Find something to applaud, even if insignificant.

One client reported to me after a week, complaining that it was too hard to find anything to praise in her son. I reassured her, saying that she would be able to find something as long as she paid close attention to her son.

Later on, she admitted that she was able to find at least one thing that she could tell her son. One day, she praised him for remembering to lock the door when leaving for school; another day, she praised him for combing his hair and dressing nicely. Then in the following week, she gave him a pat on the back for dumping the kitchen trash bin. She learned that the more closely she observed her son, the more she found good qualities. And the more goodness she found, the better her son showed up. The praises slowly changed the icy relationship between the mother and son.

My father used to tell me not only to praise my children, but to praise them lavishly. In Chinese, we need to 猛夸 for their good intentions, behaviors, or character (猛夸 means "to praise fiercely" or "to compliment excessively").

Having said that, I admit that I still do not praise my children often enough and that many Asian parents have a similar reluctance.

When my daughters got A's in school, I would think to myself, "as it should be." I didn't understand why they expected me to praise them. If they got an A- at school, that meant they did not study enough and were thus not worthy of praise. That's because Asian parents, unlike American parents, tend not to shower praise on their children even if their children have achieved something spectacular. Much of this has to do with the general belief that "谦受益、满招损," meaning "humility brings benefits, arrogance invites loss." If we praise children too much, we fear they might become vain and thereby stop improving themselves.

Also, when other parents praise our children for their achievements, we tend to humble ourselves by saying "哪里、哪里？没有的事，都是碰巧", meaning "Oh, no, no, that's not true - it was all just luck."

Please note, "哪里" literally means "where." There's a joke about "哪里." A Chinese man and his wife picked up an American businessman from the airport and treated him to a nice dinner. After the dinner, the American man thanked the man for his hospitality and praised the wife, saying "Your wife is very kind, " then added, "She's very pretty." The interpreter translated it to Chinese. The Chinese man blushed and answered "哪里、哪里". The interpreter said to the American business man, "Where, where?" The American businessman paused, thinking about the Chinese man asking him where his wife's body is pretty, and answered, "Everywhere."

So even though many Asians, and especially the Chinese, pour our heart and soul into achieving awards and recognition, we not only avoid praising our children in public, but also refuse to accept praise from others. Being praised in public can feel almost shameful—we shrink back, smile shyly, and worry others might think we're showing off, even when we're proud inside. Yes, it sounds paradoxical, but that's just the culture.

Over the years, I have learned not only to praise my children, but also accept praise from others. It does not mean they do not need to improve. When hearing compliments and admiration from others, you may just simply respond by saying "Thank you. I appreciate your support," with a big smile.

Say it Loud and Proud (Express Your Love)

For centuries, Chinese culture also discouraged the expression of affection, even between young couples. There's a saying, "爱在心头，口难开", meaning "deep love, silent tongue". Even though this tradition has changed in recent years due to Western influence, people rarely use the word "爱" ("love") in their everyday spoken language. We don't say "I love you" in Chinese to each other outside of couples, including to our parents and children.

I learned to say it after I had my first daughter. At the beginning, I only said "I love you" in English. To this day, I still feel more comfortable saying it in English to my husband, children, and parents. Saying "我爱你" (meaning "I love you") feels awkward.

My children say it with ease all the time, to their grandparents, aunt, uncle, my husband and me. They say it to their friends too. In American culture, "friends" can include nearly anyone they meet, even just once. In Chinese culture, "friend" has a much more serious connotation, meaning you commit to each other in a long term relationship. "Friends" may even die for one another.

With the ingrained cultural belief in "deep love, silent tongue," it is difficult for Chinese and other East Asian immigrants to praise our children constantly. We, as parents, seem to be able to do everything else—carry out duties and responsibilities without complaints—but somehow it feels daunting to say nice things about our children and express our appreciation for them. Instead, we are taught to respect parents, but be strict to children. That children should appreciate their parents because parents bring up children and raise them with sacrifice. Not the other way around.

Before arriving in America, my generation had already absorbed Western values and images from movies, literature, and music. We knew that Americans showed appreciation to their children by saying "Thank you. Please. I love you. You are precious. I'm grateful for you." Even after reaching American shores, I still found these expressions surprising. Eventually, however, I joined "those parents" who show affection to their children.

That's when my children were young. Saying "I love you" became harder as they grew older and talked back during arguments. If it's difficult enough for at least second-generation American parents who may feel frustrated with frequent conflicts, it is even harder for immigrant parents from East Asia.

A friend of mine recently shared a most useful "weapon" during a heated conversation: three simple words— "I love you". In family arguments, there's rarely a clear right or wrong, because family isn't a courtroom or a debate stage. It's not about logic, evidence, or proving a point. The line between right and wrong is often blurry and smooshy. It's not about winning, but about feeling seen, heard, and nurtured. Saying "I love you" helps melt the ice in our hearts.

Saying "I love you" is one of the most meaningful deposits we can make into our children's Emotional Bank. And this bank matters more than we realize.

Emotional Bank

I learned the term "Emotional Bank" from *The Seven Habits of Highly Effective People* by Stephen Covey in 2010, a book I had won from a competition hosted by Young Professionals Network at Wells Fargo where I was working (Covey 1989, 215). This was the same period I decided to improve my public speaking and leadership skills. I never imagined that *The Seven Habits* would provide not only a lasting impact on growth at work, but also on life in general.

One concept that stuck with me was the "Emotional Bank Account." Covey explains that every relationship functions like a bank account (Covey 1989, 215). When we do something that builds trust or makes another person feel valued, we make a deposit. When we let them down, hurt them, or break trust, we make a withdrawal. Over time, the balance determines the strength of the relationship.

I had never heard of it, but it later made sense to me. When I praised my children for their character or behavior, they smiled at me and were happy to follow my suggestions. But if I yelled at them for their shortcomings or mistakes, they rebelled and opposed my suggestions.

Of course, I am not pretending that our relationships with our children can be as neatly configured as the deposits, withdrawals, and interest in our bank accounts. But it's a handy metaphor for us to remember because it reminds us of something simple: every word and action either builds trust or erodes it. The more "deposits" we make with kindness, respect, and encouragement, the stronger the relationship grows.

I was struck by a story a friend told me about an old man she knew for some time. Originally from China, the man was very successful and wealthy. He worked hard, invested smartly, and accumulated enough assets to retire early. His only regret was that his adult son refused to talk to him for several years. The man felt lonely after his wife passed away, lamenting that he would probably die alone one day.

Although my friend did not know the entire story, what I gleaned from the details was that the man was very harsh to his son during the latter's childhood. Using the concept of the emotional bank, the old man withdrew all of the money from the bank, leaving nothing, or even a negative balance. You see, the son had completely cut all ties off with his father.

Everyone in our circle who heard about the story sighed and felt sorry for the old man. Perhaps the old man regretted that he damaged the relationship by scolding or neglecting his son so harshly and making his childhood and adolescence miserable. If the old man could only lower his head and apologize to his son, that would be a deposit in the emotional bank.

This reminded me of another story that I read on social media a few years ago. A young woman saved the sticky notes from her stepfather for years. Not only did she make a board with the sticky notes, but also framed it and sent it to him as a Father's Day gift. When her stepfather opened the gift and saw the picture of him holding her in his arms in the center of the board with numerous yellow sticky notes surrounding the picture, he was in awe. Speechless, he covered his mouth with his hand and cried. The daughter rubbed his shoulder saying, "These are your notes… I kept them all. Happy Father's Day!" These encouraging notes were written by her stepfather every day before school, helping her through tough times in middle school and high school. I could not restrain my tears when I watched the video clip and read the story (Yoder 2019).

I heard a similar story from a friend about a mother who wrote a sticky note to her 12-year-old son and put it in his lunch box every day to encourage him. Even though the boy refused to talk to his mother for several days because of depression, she did not give up. She wrote an endearing sentence every day, hoping he would respond to her.

Day after day, the son remained silent, and the mother thought the son might be tired of seeing the notes and stopped writing. One day, she saw him searching for something in the kitchen after coming home from school. When asked, the son replied, "Where is your note?" The mother then realized that she forgot to put the note in that morning. She hugged her son and took out the note from her pocket. The son obviously cared and cherished the note. That's the power of love.

My father used to write a birthday card to each of my daughters on their birthday from an early age, before they ever learned to read. He insisted on giving them a card with a blessing and good wishes while inserting a red envelope with money. I did not think it was necessary because they were too young, and it was not until they were older that they began caring about the red envelope.

In the last few years before my father passed away, he no longer remembered their birthdays due to his dementia, so he stopped giving them birthday cards and red envelopes. One day, my second daughter showed me all of the cards that my father gave her, saying "How I wish Laoye still gave me cards!" (Laoye means grandpa in Chinese.) I suddenly realized that young children can remember and cherish loving gestures. Each time I helped them read the card, his words took root in their hearts. My daughters never forgot the cards: that's also the power of love.

In my youngest daughter's junior and senior year at high school, she struggled a lot with academic pressure, college applications, my mom's passing, allergies, and friendship challenges. While trying to spend more time with her and not add more pressure, I wrote numerous cards with warm messages, including one month when I wrote one card per day. On those days when she closed her door and refused to talk to anyone, I put my card next to her food on the kitchen counter so that she could see it easily.

I would praise her in each card, telling her that I love her. Sometimes, I would tell her, "You are so kind. You are so capable." At other times, I would write, "You are smart. You are blessed. You are talented. I'm proud of you. You are my sunshine." At the bottom of the card, I would draw my smiley face next to "Love, Mom." I used these cards to win back my daughter's smiles many times. Sometimes, she did not respond to me, while on other days, she would quietly give me a hug.

I encourage all parents to find a way to deposit love into their children's emotional bank. It's never too late to say nice things about your children to their faces. It's one of the best ways to strengthen the relationship, helping them recognize their value and thereby enhancing their self image both of which serve as the foundation of confidence and resilience. They will learn how and where to seek comfort whenever embroiled in any crisis.

Exercises

1. Express your love: Say "I love you" every day.
2. Smile at your child: Look into their eyes and smile daily.
3. Hug your child: Even a gentle pat on the shoulder counts—do it every day.
4. Praise their inner beauty and essence while acknowledging their character daily.
5. Compliment their appearance and good deeds every day.

6. Praise them in their presence: Compliments shared directly with them are more impactful than those mentioned behind their back.
7. Replace giving commands with open-ended questions (e.g. what, when, who, how, and why)
8. Pray for your child: Do it in front of them and also in private.

Chapter 5

Principle 2: Redefine Success

"Success is not the key to happiness. Happiness is the key to success."
— ALBERT SCHWEITZER

大器晚成 is a Chinese idiom from Laozi. It means "A great vessel takes time to be made." A great vessel requires more time to craft than a simple one, just as a person with significant potential may take longer to achieve success. Examples throughout history show that success is not solely determined by early academic achievement; there are at least as many examples of those who succeed otherwise.

What is success? It's a varying term for many people. There are many successful people around the world and far too many books that teach you how to become "successful." But, what does it actually mean? Each person has their own definition. Most people associate it with fame and fortune. But to others, it can mean being healthy or living a purposeful life.

Many parents want to raise a successful child in the conventional sense of the term—wealthy, accomplished, and perhaps famous. These expectations may begin from an early age with parents anxiously hoping for a child who is strong, healthy, happy, independent, and capable. When such criteria are mostly present in a child, parents feel hopeful, reaching for the next goal: academic performance.

But for parents raising a child with neurodivergence, a disability, or developmental delays, success can mean different things. Success might look like seeing their child overcome daily hurdles, finding joy in small moments, or experiencing life with confidence and dignity. Their version of success usually isn't tied to grades, but rooted in love, patience, and the quiet wins of everyday progress.

In this chapter, I explore the key components of success beyond health and social well-being: college, money, and books. To me, these represent the pillars of growth and opportunity because education shapes your future, financial literacy builds independence, and reading fuels lifelong learning.

You Are Unique, But Not Special (Lower Your Expectations)

Holding my first daughter in my arms when she was only a few weeks old, such a tiny creature, I couldn't help but dream about her future.

"She must be so smart, a genius. What's the word? Prodigy?" I thought.

"Will she become a top scientist? An extraordinary artist? An outstanding world leader?" I fell in love with my own expectations.

Don't laugh at me. There are more parents than you might imagine who share the same outlandish dreams for their children. I heard a joke about a woman's dream. First, the woman dreamed of becoming an outstanding leader herself and making an impact. Eventually, she abandoned this thought as reality set in. Then, she dreamed of marrying someone outstanding instead. After marriage, she realized that her husband was just an ordinary man. So, she decided to give birth to an outstanding hero. She placed her high hopes on her child.

Tiger Mothers always expect so much from their children. That's because as immigrants, especially those of us who did not grow up with abundant resources, we want our children to achieve even more than we have as we expect one generation to outdo the previous one. Having uprooted ourselves from familiar cultures and environments and succeeding in this country after overcoming so many obstacles, we all but expect our children to exceed our achievements in a better environment. After all, for many immigrants, this desire to have our children live up to the best expectations is one of the main reasons for settling down in America.

There's nothing wrong with parents wanting to see their children become great leaders and outstanding figures. However, expectations should be realistic, supportive, and adaptable. After all, successive generations do not necessarily always outperform earlier ones: this is a fact of life that we see all around the world. The goal is to nurture confidence, independence, and self-worth, not just achievements. A child needs to feel supported rather than pressured.

Over the years, I have realized that yes, my children are unique, rather than special, because they have their own personalities, talents, and hobbies. Too many parents, however, fail to make the distinction between unique and special. Think about it: if every child is special, then no one is special. And even if your child is a prodigy, it's important to temper your expectations.

As mentioned in the previous chapter, when parents place too much hope on a child, seeing them as their only hope, the child can feel suffocated—and the parents may feel overwhelmed as well.

Do not define their achievements as your only hope, success, and reputation. Your worth does not depend on others' achievements, nor your children's. You are good enough.

When you shift your expectations, your happiness will return. This means letting go of comparisons or judging your parenting skills based on how closely your children's accomplishments align with your expectations. You will become more relaxed, as will your body. The best thing you can do is enjoy the existence and companionship of your child.

In Chinese, we have a popular saying, "不以成败论英雄", meaning "A true hero is not judged solely by success or failure". The origin of the idiom came from the true story of Yue Fei, a famous general in the Song Dynasty. He was known for his patriotism and leading an army to resist foreign invaders. While betrayed by his own people prior to imprisonment and execution, he is considered one of the true heroes in Chinese history because worth is not defined by winning or losing.

We should also remind ourselves that our children have their own course of life that may or may not meet your expectations. They may have different talents and interests in addition to different experiences in life as an Asian growing up in the U.S. (or really, anywhere in the West.)

I have learned that I should not expect my children to respond to my suggestions right away. Even if I don't see anything wrong with my opinions, I now realize my children see things in a completely different light because of our different experiences.

Remember that your children have their own ideas and they will be the ones attending the college in question, not you. While your suggestions matter to them, they may feel inclined to make decisions their own way given their experience and circumstances.

Here are some reminders you should bear in mind when you are feeling ever so vaguely dissatisfied. Tell yourself:

- "My child is doing just fine."
- "I'm grateful she's healthy."
- "She's my child. She seems stubborn—probably because she has my genes."
- "She wants to run her own way. I'm glad she wants to be independent."
- "That she has her own ideas means I can relax."
- "She will grow eventually."
- "She's young. She needs time. I'm not expecting too much."

Yes, You Need to Go to College (College - A Never Ending Topic)

Education is an extremely important cultural concern in China and other Asian countries, one that dates back to the history of the Imperial Examination System (科举制度) of over one thousand years in China. It was a system used to select government officials based on exams and played a crucial role in shaping Chinese society, governance, and education. Becoming a government official brought wealth and power to the individual and family.

For many poor families, getting good scores was the only means to greater wealth and a higher social status. That's a mentality that has persisted through the centuries. College entrance exams in modern China still rank among the most rigorous exams in the world.

Given this mindset, it is not surprising that many Chinese immigrants—and Indians too—have achieved high academic success. These individuals are often selected by top U.S. colleges and awarded scholarships, enabling them to obtain student visas that they otherwise wouldn't be able to obtain. They are also hired by American companies, securing work visas that allow them to build their careers in the U.S.

For these immigrants, academic excellence serves as the key to opportunity, opening doors to jobs, financial stability, and a future in America. Naturally, they aspire for their children to follow in their footsteps, believing that success in academics leads to success in life.

College is a never-ending topic among immigrant parents. The mindset is not only "Yes, my child, you need to go to college," but also "you need to go to a prestigious college!" Pressure from Chinese parents begins at an early age as they push for top grades. The goal is for their children to eventually attend a good college—ideally, an Ivy League or Ivy plus school.

As such, parents usually rush their children to attend various afterschool programs before steering them to SAT/ACT prep courses, private tutors, and private college counselors when they reach high school, if not earlier. Not surprisingly, they are willing to pay hefty amounts of money for these programs.

Offering the best higher education to their children usually involves financial sacrifices, especially if the university in question costs nearly $100,000 a year exclusive of other living expenses. This is one of the reasons why Asian parents care less about buying the latest model car or expensive clothes when they anticipate the high costs of attending college. Most parents in my circle, myself included, chose to pay tuition fees in full rather than letting their children carry student loans. This is why I would like to suggest that Chinese parents discuss college choices with their children and let them make the decision. Going to an expensive school is not the only way for children to be successful.

There are several factors for parents to consider when planning for college for their child.

First of all, going to college is a privilege particularly when tuition, room and board, and other costs are out of limits for many families. Parents need to manage their expectations ahead of time while communicating them to their child.

Secondly, parents may stress the importance of getting higher education, but they should let their children decide how to pursue it. Put them in the driver's seat, just as if they were learning to drive.

This is where a college counselor comes in handy. A counselor can offer expertise, guidance, and emotional support in the application process, providing your child agrees to getting outside help. They can help with finding appropriate colleges, financial aid packages, and sometimes test and essay coaching.

For example, one friend told me she deeply appreciated her daughter's counselor because of the emotional support provided during the extremely stressful application process. Another parent shared that having a counselor helped her avoid friction at home since her suggestions were better received when they came through a neutral third party. One mother said the greatest benefit was simply keeping her daughter on track with deadlines and that's something she could never do due to her own busy schedule.

Nonetheless, you should also be aware that hiring an expensive college counselor can add additional expectations for your child. Command Education, a college admission consulting firm, is reported to charge $120,000 for one-year consulting packages (Chen 2024). In my circle, I've seen parents pay $5,000-$15,000 to college admission counselors for several months to help their children apply for college.

The reality, however, is that admissions to top schools such as Ivy League universities is notoriously difficult, with many comparing it to a lottery. Some research has shown that admissions for Asians is more limited in comparison to that for white students. For instance, Asian American applicants had 28% lower odds of attending an Ivy-11 school compared to similarly qualified White applicants (Grossman, et al. 2024). Finally, there's the fact that elite colleges also favor wealthy students even when their grades are no better than those of students from a middle or working class background (Cooper 2023).

This is why I suggest parents view college admissions from the perspective of their children. Is attending a top college the only way of attaining success for the present and future? Although there is no doubt that admission to a prestigious university conveys intelligence, it is important to remember that many paths to fame and fortune do not necessarily require a degree from such an institution. One study revealed that many top corporate executives do not have Ivy degrees; if anything, the most common attainment is the lack of a college degree (Shin 2023).

And of course, we've all heard success stories of college dropouts starting up a company and becoming innovative entrepreneurs. Obviously, not every dropout can succeed as phenomenally as Steve Jobs, Bill Gates, and Mark Zuckerberg. But not attending college does not mean that they will become a failure in life either. They may also learn a great deal outside of the classroom or gain a better sense of their interests and talents before returning to college later in life. The fact is life is not a straight line. Parents should aim to be open minded about their children's choices and allow them to soar in their own fashion.

So even though I urged my children to go to college, explaining that "going to college gives you more opportunities to learn and grow," I left the choice of college up to them. After all, *they* would be attending college, not me.

Once their children attend college, Asian parents also tend to steer their children into certain fields, with the most common being computer science, electrical engineering, data science, medicine, and accounting. Some students enjoy these fields and that's fine. But other students may not be as interested or have different talents and skills: as we saw earlier, conflicts over careers can destroy family relationships. This is where parents need to think about the long term effects of these stipulated studies on their children. Will their son or daughter feel intellectually or emotionally fulfilled? We often overlook the fact that other paths in skilled manual labor are also stable, well-paying, and fulfilling: after all, everyone will need a plumber, electrician, or technician.

Success can come in different ways. Simu Liu, who played the protagonist in *Shang-Chi and the Legend of the Ten Rings*, shared his struggle with his parents in his book *We Were Dreamers: An Immigrant Superhero Origin Story*. He mentioned that his parents, both engineers, emphasized the importance of science and mathematics, urging him toward what they regarded as a stable profession. He said, "I had only been exposed to the straight-and-narrow way: go to school, get a degree, graduate, get a job, make money, buy a house, and then die" (Liu 2023, 196). He followed the path that his parents designed for him - studied accounting and landed a job at Deloitte. After being laid off, he decided to follow his passion for acting, eventually

leading to his role as Shang-Chi in the Marvel
Cinematic Universe.

Therefore, parents need to allow their children to
decide the major. Choosing a hot major does not
guarantee success, particularly when the job market is
changing more rapidly than ever: computer science, for
instance, has been losing popularity with changes in
technology and the rise of AI (Horowitch 2025). So
don't worry if they don't have a clear picture of what to
study. As it is, an increasing number of adults switch
careers and that is a significant difference from their
parents. I myself changed from environmental
engineering to financial data analysis to risk
management. And now, I am an executive coach and
author.

Equally important is consideration of your children's
mental and physical health. Far too many Asian
students are snapping under the burden of unrealistic
standards, with some suffering an inferiority complex,
believing they are never good enough, nervous
breakdowns, or in worst case scenarios, committing
suicide. In fact, The Centers for Disease Control and
Prevention (CDC) reported that in 2021, suicide was
the third leading cause of death among U.S. high
school youth aged 14-18 years with the rate of 9 per
100,000 youths (Verlenden, et al. 2024).

Studies from the Association for Child and Adolescent Mental Health have also shown that the suicide rate of Asian Americans and Pacific Islanders doubled from 3.6 to 7.1 per 100,000 during 1999-2021, thus emphasizing the importance of mental health support (Reyes, et al. 2024). This is why parents need to check on their children to ensure they are not feeling unduly pressured by high expectations and excessive work loads. So much for dreams of success and happiness! In Chinese, we say "本末倒置", meaning "putting the cart before the horse." Such can only destroy the relationship between parents and children.

Again, attending a particular college is not the single important determining factor for a child's future success. The more important thing for parents to remember is to allow their children to make their own decisions and goals. For instance, how important is wealth? Independence? More importantly, how do their skills, talents, temperament align with their passions?

Money Is Important And Necessary—but not everything

When we define success, we usually think of wealth first. We admire those executives and entrepreneurs who earn millions, if not billions, of dollars and consider them to be successful. As parents, we praise and envy those children who graduate from a good college and find a lucrative job. But we should also agree that competing over wealth is fruitless because there are always going to be others who inherit or earn more.

A worthier goal would entail the encouragement of financial independence and the acceptance of professional challenges involved with certain studies and careers.

Although this book is not intended to teach parents and children financial literacy or financial planning techniques since that could easily occupy an entire book, I'd like to focus on less talked about but equally important issues.

First, help your children understand the meaning of money.

Immigrant parents tend to be very frugal, saving every dollar for their house, car, and children's education. That is why they generally have lower levels of debt than native-born Americans (Alvarez 2019).

There are, no doubt, advantages to managing money economically and effectively. You can begin by teaching them that money does not fall from the sky. Earning money means hard work and dedication. It also means blessing and privilege. Parents' money is not automatically their children's. Children also need to work hard to earn their own money.

At the same time, we also need to teach children to understand the true worth of money: namely, that money is a vehicle to more choices and freedom. While important, however, it is not *the* most important thing in life. If you define money as success, then your children will chase after money. That is sometimes to the detriment of their personal happiness or ironically enough, success.

That's why it's crucial to allow children to manage their money. During Chinese New Year, we have a tradition of giving red envelopes to children. Some parents will collect money from their children's red envelopes for fear that their children will misuse the money. Some do so in order to save money for future usage, such as college, piano lessons, etc.

I suggest that parents not worry about the misuse and instead allow children to learn to manage their money. Parents may ask the children how to spend their money and make suggestions. Even if they misuse their money, they are better off learning the lesson now rather than later.

Third, teach children to give and share wisely. Long ago, I heard from friends that the Jewish religion and culture recommends giving 10% of income to charitable causes. Even though I did not grow up with this tradition as a Chinese immigrant, I have learned to make donations over the years. Teaching children to save, share, and give wisely is one of the most meaningful lessons parents can pass on.

In 2008, Wenchuan County in Sichuan Province, China, experienced a disastrous earthquake where at least 69,195 people were killed (National Centers for Environmental Information 2025). The world responded with an outpouring of aid. At that time, my oldest daughter was in an elementary school in the Bay Area. Her school quickly raised $200 within one week. One boy donated $80, which was his entire birthday gift. I was so inspired seeing little children jumping in to help. Behind that boy's selfless act were parents who had nurtured a spirit of giving. Teaching children to contribute from a young age helps them understand that money is more than a tool for making a living—it is also a way to build community and to honor the gift of life through helping others.

When we talk about success, true success must be built on purpose and values.

Read, Read, Read (life-long learning).

I cannot sufficiently emphasize the importance of helping children to read more because it's a means to lifelong learning and curiosity.

Reading is arguably one of the best habits of all times. It opens the world to the reader and allows the reader to have imagination and experience the life they would not otherwise have. In Chinese, we say, "书中自有黄金屋，书中自有颜如玉", meaning there are gold houses and beautiful girls in books. People who love reading tend to have a broader view about life and the world around them. Encouraging children to read from a young age helps parents to have a better understanding between each other and resolving conflict.

Books are the bridges between family members and people growing up from different environments. A friend of mine told me that she would always ask her son what book he was reading before borrowing the same book from the library. She read what her son read, so that she would understand his views and emotions. She said that encouraging her son to read from a young age was the best thing she had done for him. Whenever there's a conflict, she would think of the book and find a useful quote or story to share with her son.

Reading books help people to learn and grow. Tai Lopez, an entrepreneur in multiple industries including e-commerce and real estates shared how reading a book (or parts of a book) every day exposed him to the wisdom of others, accelerated his learning, and transformed his personal and professional life. He attributed his success to this daily habit, observing that the success of a person in five years will be based on two things: the books read and the people around them. Book reading not only exposes new ideas, but also cultivates lifelong learning and curiosity. Furthermore, it's an important part of personal growth and character building. At the end of the day, success is not only measured by wealth, social status, but also by continuous exploration and growth.

Ultimately, a great vessel takes time to be crafted. True success is not about rushing or achieving milestones quickly; it is about continuous growth, resilience, and lifelong learning. As parents, our role is not to push our children toward high test scores or prestigious colleges but to cultivate an environment that nurtures curiosity, self-confidence, and a love for learning. When we shift away from a scarcity mindset, we recognize that success is not limited to a select few; rather, it is something that each person can define and achieve in their own way and time.

This is why parents should engage in meaningful conversations with their children about what success truly means and guide them toward a fulfilling and balanced life. Beyond academic achievements, a successful person is someone who is healthy, engaged in meaningful work, financially stable, and surrounded by supportive relationships. These are the foundations of a well-rounded and rewarding life.

A friend of mine once said, "A successful child is not just one who excels in school but one who, by the age of 35, is healthy, independent, and has built a loving family and fulfilling relationships. Only then can a parent truly be called successful."

Rather than chasing short-term victories, let's focus on helping our children build the mindset, skills, and character that will serve them for a lifetime. Success is not a race to the finish line—it is a journey of growth, discovery, and purpose.

Exercises

1. Redefining success for family
   - Write down the top 5 definitions of success and discuss it with children (e.g. health, career, relationship, financial independence, etc.)
   - For parents, ask yourself, "Is my current focus on grades and other external achievements helping or hindering my child's overall development?"

2. Creating an Environment for Lifelong Learning
   - List three ways you can support your child's curiosity outside of academic achievement.
   - Parents may ask themselves, "How can I nurture my child's passion for learning in everyday life?"

3. Family Success Vision Board
    - Invite each family member to work on their own vision board for the year or semester.
    - Invite everyone to work together on a family vision board.
    - Share and display the vision boards

Chapter 6

Principle 3: Let Them ~~Fail~~ Fly

I was standing by the classroom window, watching the raindrops splashing on the glass and breaking into tiny dots. It was 1981, and I was 11. The wind pushed and swung the tree branches around as they tried to cling to the trunk without snapping off. I was hoping the storm would stop, at least before 5 o'clock. But, instead, it gathered enough strength to continue for the whole afternoon.

By the time the school day ended, the rain was still pouring like an unstoppable waterfall. As the classroom door opened, a father poked his head into the classroom, glancing through the room. All heads turned as one student suddenly jumped out of his seat and dashed toward his father. All of the other kids gazed at the student enviously before turning their heads back to the window to continue watching the downpour. Everyone wished their parents would show up soon.

Back then, no families owned a car. Being picked up by your parents meant you still had to walk home, but at least with an umbrella and a warm hand holding your cold hand. If you were lucky enough, your parents could put you on their bike.

I sat at my desk, anxiously waiting for the next parent. *Where's Mom? Would she show up at all, somehow miraculously?* She never picked me up from school, whether it was hot, cold, sunny, or stormy. And now, here I was, virtually alone as my classmates were picked up one-by-one by their parents with an umbrella in hand.

I sighed and lost hope. I was among the last few students whose parents did not show up.

It was 5:00 pm. The rain just kept pouring. After watching the rain for another fifteen minutes, I decided to walk home. Fortunately, the rain had turned to a light patter. The raindrops on my face felt soft, even soothing. After all, it was spring when temperatures were just beginning to rise.

Even though I practically ran home most of the way, clutching my backpack tightly to keep my books dry, I still arrived home soaking wet. I was the first one back in the house in the evening. As I waited for my mother and brother (my father worked in another city), I removed my wet clothes and put on dry and clean ones before handwashing the wet clothes. Because there were no washing machines before 1980, I learned to wash my clothes when I was six.

I then prepared some rice soup for dinner.

Sometimes, I wished I had a "better" mother and even suspected that she was not related to me whenever she scolded me. She was nearly the opposite of Dad, who always spoke gently to me and forgave my mistakes.

I couldn't help but notice that Mom was not like other mothers who sewed new clothes for my friends. She could not cook to save her life, although I suspect she was hardly interested in housework.

Nonetheless, I missed her presence as I sat in my favorite comfy chair. I loved listening to her singing. Her skill was unrivaled, and she had what I considered the most beautiful voice in the world.

Mom finally came home from work, soaked through as well. She tried to catch her breath.

"Great, you are home!" Her face was red as her eyes sparkled.

"Mom, I walked home in the rain," I stood tall and straight. I was already taller than she was.

"Very good!" She glanced at me and put down her bag.

She wrapped a dry towel around her head, rubbing her head vigorously as if to remove every drop of water. After changing, she rushed to the kitchen to make dinner, humming all the way. She did not even ask me how I made it home by myself; I wanted to tell her about how I had slipped and tumbled on the muddy road. I followed her into the kitchen.

"Mom, why do you never pick me up from school?" I pouted, feeling neglected.

She turned to me. "I had to finish my lab work before leaving." Pausing, she added, "You look dry. That's good. I'm glad you changed into dry clothes."

She smiled at me.

"Why do you never pick me up from school?" I pressed further.

"I believe that you can handle everything yourself. You are such a capable girl," she answered, looking into my eyes. "You are brave and strong. I'm very proud of you."

She patted my head and said, "Rain makes you stronger. You need it," then went back to humming.

Dinner that night was delicious, with the vegetable dishes Mom cooked and the rice soup I made.

Many years later, I learned the Chinese phrase "没伞的孩子跑得更快," meaning "Youths without umbrellas ran faster." I was the child without an umbrella, since Mom taught me to rely upon myself at an early age. Having lost both parents during World War II at the age of four, Mom had to figure out everything on her own. With no mother to care for her and teach her to cook, sew, or clean, she learned basic living skills by observing others and by practicing. And as such, she also went from being a poor orphan in a farmer's family to a high-achieving physicist at a national research institute.

Mom passed away in October 2024, at the age of 86. What did I learn from her? I've asked myself that question many times. Besides her love, she taught me countless skills, values, and her characteristic traits, of which two of the most important were optimism and pliability.

"You will figure it out, my child," she would always tell me, smiling.

She knew that I was able to figure out solutions, like how to walk home safely in the rain. I learned to watch the sky, calculate the safest and shortest route home, assess the best time to start running, avoid slippery and muddy roads, take cover under overhanging roofs, and pick myself up after falling down. I learned to clutch my books, shielding them from the rain. I learned to change my wet clothes and wash them for the next day.

And so I learned to appreciate Mom for not picking me up from school that day and many days after. I learned to appreciate not becoming a delicate flower protected in a greenhouse, but a tree standing tall and firm in the rain. I learned to manage in storms and wind, sometimes falling down, but always getting up while wiping off the tears and dirt.

There's a new trend in parenting today—FAFO, meaning "fxxx around and find out." Though seemingly callous, there's an important message here: let your child take risks when necessary. Don't try to protect them 24/7. Just tell them that rain makes them stronger and you are there to cheer them on.

Let them Fail

When I suggest "Let them fail" to parents, their pupils enlarge and mouths open. Then they inhale.

"How can we let them fail?" They look—or even shout—in disbelief.

My first disclaimer is that letting their children fail does not mean that parents do not step in when terrible things are happening, such as in cases of self-harm, aggression, or playing with fire—whether literally or figuratively. "Let them fail" simply means that we allow our children to make mistakes and learn from their failures. So while we observe and coach our children, they will still take full responsibility for their actions. In this way, they can grow more confident and resilient.

We all know that we grow more during challenging times. All of the wins and achievements help us feel good, but the losses can teach us far more about life. I still remember all my woefully imperfect presentations, client complaints, and critical conversations with my bosses. From those experiences, I gained more knowledge and experience on risk management, credit management, and lending practices.

As parents, we tend to forget our own learning process and want to rectify our children's lives at the slightest mishap. Here are my suggestions:

1. Remain calm when "bad" things happen to your child, e.g. they failed a test, lost a friendship, or got teased.
2. Do not criticize or ridicule them.
3. Watch and listen to their side of the story and struggles.
4. Ask open-ended questions instead of intervening immediately.
5. Offer help when they seek our opinions.
6. Warn them about their choices, but don't threaten them.
7. Help them to reflect on what they have learned from their mistakes.

Let them Grow

We all understand that each person is different with their own characteristics and talents—just like different flowers blossom at different times. Each child has their own course to learn and grow. Some begin talking at the age of one, while others do not talk until they are three or four.

According to my parents, I started talking when I was not even one. My very first story included only three words, "wolf", "five-money", and "brother". The story was based on a news report on the radio, which was the only source of entertainment, since practically no one in China had a TV back in the 1970s. A little boy living in a mountain area found a wounded animal and rescued it. He couldn't figure out what it was, since it resembled a wolf as much as a leopard. The next day, he brought the leopard-wolf creature to an animal research institute, asking for help and further information.

Surprisingly, the animal was an endangered leopard. The government rewarded the little boy with a significant sum, but the boy refused to accept it, saying he had done the right thing. I was fascinated by the news, trying to retell the story to everyone. I called that little boy, "brother", that leopard "wolf", and the reward money "five-money" since "five" sounded a lot. This experience led my mom to praise me for a special talent in storytelling.

But I had my own deficiencies too, including frequent illnesses. I could not participate in playground activities such as rotating chairs and slides. I was always the slowest and clumsiest among my friends. Nonetheless, my mother was never terribly worried even if it was not easy to raise me. She would say, "Small sprouts will eventually grow (有苗不愁长)." She explained that nature would guide my growth. I eventually grew stronger and taller.

If a child is meeting most standard expectations for their age, there's no need to worry excessively about their physical or mental growth. Unfortunately today, parents are too anxious in their desire for an outstanding child. Being born is already evidence of a child's strength in the natural selection process. The idea that "不让孩子输在起跑线上", which translates to "do not let your child lose at the beginning of the race", has become popularized in recent years. Far too many parents seem to believe that the child will be doomed for failure if not provided with the best tutoring and education from kindergarten.

I used to worry about the ranking of my daughter's elementary school many years ago when she was only a kindergartner. I clearly remember her teacher smiling at me, saying "She'll be fine. She's clever."

Nonetheless, I still transferred her to a better school.

As it turned out, both schools were nearly identical, with only a one point difference in ranking.

Asian entrepreneur Dave Lu observes that many immigrant parents raise their children according to the values and survival mindset shaped by their own upbringing. While rooted in cultural tradition, this approach passes down a scarcity mindset which is unduly shaped by fear, limitation, and a survival mindset (Lu 2023).

Growing up as the son of parents who immigrated to the US in the 1960s, Lu fully understood his parents' reliance on a security-driven survival ethos. While appreciating his parents' efforts, he chose to reshape his own mindset by breaking the "bamboo ceiling" and starting his own company. But he did not stop there. He became more vocal, advocating for the Asian Pacific Islander community to shift their mindset from scarcity to abundance.

His experience highlights an important fact for immigrant parents—our fears are real, but we do not need to let the fears set the pace of our children's growth.

Several suggestions for parents:

1. Believe that your child is resilient by nature.
2. Your child has their own timing for learning things: there is no need to pressure them.
3. Encourage your child to develop their own interests.
4. Offer help, but give them full control, since it's part of their growth process. Remember they are players on the field and you are coaches on the sidelines. Your coaching and encouragement are the support they need.
5. Allow your children to have their space to think and reflect.
6. Respect their decisions even if they are totally wrong in your eyes.

7. Teach them to relax and handle difficult
   situations calmly.

There's a Chinese saying, "不听老人言，吃亏在眼前",
meaning "If you don't listen to the old man's words, you
will suffer the consequences in front of you." Since we
are experienced, we want our children to follow us so
that they can enjoy a shortcut.

But even with all of the best wishes, our children may
not choose to listen to us. That is totally fine. Just like
how we sometimes ignored our parents when they
nagged us, our children will most likely do the same: in
fact, it's part of the learning process. It's not that they
do not value our input. They just want to learn how to
make decisions in their lives because they want to be as
independent as you. So, my suggestion is that we may
need to stand back more often than not.

Let them Watch

As I mentioned previously, letting them fail and grow
does not mean that we do not interfere when the
situation is beyond their control. When things truly go
wrong or safety is at risk, it's our responsibility to step in.
That's the right moment to don our "Superman" or
"Wonder Woman" cape. We teach them that we
protect out of love, not for control.

One of my closest friends, Amy, told me how she helped her 13-year-old daughter Belle navigate a challenging time in middle school. Belle was a bookworm and loved English literature. However, she had started skipping homework assignments for several weeks. When asked, she kept quiet. Besides reminding Belle to make up homework, Amy did not care that much, allowing her to handle it.

One day, Amy received a letter from the school informing her of Belle's misbehavior. Amy decided to ask Belle first that night.

Belle's immediate answer was, "It must be my English teacher. She hates me and I hate her."

No wonder Belle hadn't finished her English homework. That was unusual for her because English had been her favorite subject since she was young.

"What happened between you and her?" Amy asked Belle.

"Nothing. It's just that she hates me." Belle turned her back to Amy.

"You need to tell me what has happened in the classroom and I can help you," Amy walked closer to Belle and looked her in the eye.

After a while, Belle finally admitted to her mom that she mocked her English teacher's voice during break and drew a picture of her teacher with a witch hat.

She added, "I did nothing wrong… We all hate the book she chose - it was not age appropriate."

Amy was surprised by her daughter's disrespectful behavior, but she was also curious about the book. After getting the title of the book, she researched the book fully, including book reviews.

It turned out that her daughter was right about the book. There were plenty of mixed reviews, including a lot of comments in line with Belle's assessment. Amy collected the negative comments about the book into a Word document.

On the day of meeting the school counselors, she apologized for her daughter's behavior, then presented her findings and explained the reason behind Belle's resistance. She requested that they review her findings thoroughly after the meeting and to consider removing the book from the curriculum.

The school counselors agreed to her request while adding that they had no authority to change the curriculum for the current semester. They also suggested she contact the school district's curriculum office for future planning.

Amy did not stop there. She wrote a lengthy email, providing reasons for her opposition to the book before copying it to the school district superintendent.

Throughout the entire process, Amy remained calm, at least in front of her daughter Belle. Of course, Amy felt uncomfortable because as an immigrant, she was unfamiliar not only with American culture but also the middle school education system. She did not know whom to contact and how to protect her daughter's rights. But her maternal instinct drove her to take her daughter's side. She spent the whole week consulting with other parents, searching for answers online, and researching the book. Belle watched her mom fight hard for her concerns.

The end result? It took the school district some time to process the recommendation. Two years later, Amy found out that the book finally became an optional book for the 8th grade classes. Five years later, the book was removed from the curriculum. It was a long wait, but worth the effort.

The key is to find a balance between excessive involvement and neglect. Parents need to understand the right time of involvement to protect their little ones. Be a model for them and trust they will follow you, even if not right away. Parents' actions will make a long-lasting impact on their children. Let them watch you.

Exercises

1. Reflect on the following questions:
   a. What are some ways you can allow your child to take on more responsibility while still providing guidance?
   b. How do you define resilience? How has your definition evolved over time?

2. Rate yourself (1-5, with 5 being the highest) on the following statements:
   a. I allow my child (or someone I mentor) to make mistakes and learn from them.
   b. I stay calm when things go wrong instead of immediately stepping in.
   c. I model resilience and problem-solving for my children/students rather than just instructing them.
   d. I encourage independence by letting children handle tasks on their own.

   For any score below a 3, write down one action you can take to improve in that area.

3. Choose one task this week that you typically do for your child and let them handle it instead. Observe how they respond, and resist the urge to interfere unless absolutely necessary.

Chapter 7

Principle 4: Show, ~~But~~ Not And Tell

"I praise you so you'll know you're capable. I set rules so you'll know which way to go… A parent should be steady and gentle, not harsh."
— My father

EQ Is More Important (EQ vs IQ)

We all know that both IQ (intelligence quotient) and EQ (emotional quotient) are important factors in success. Compared to IQ, however, EQ can play a larger and more long-term role in a person's career and personal life. In an era that requires close collaboration and teamwork, EQ is a necessary component of communication and leadership skills. In other words, we want our children to possess social as much as cognitive smarts.

While many Asian parents stress the importance of IQ and academic achievement, they should also learn that EQ is at least as crucial for happiness, relationships, and leadership skills.

But in order to teach these skills, we need to learn and practice them first.

By far, the most crucial skill is learning how to remain calm. The Chinese have a saying that "a mother's calmness is a child's blessing." When we keep calm and handle our emotions properly, our children feel safe and stable because there's always a solution.

Imagine a sudden crisis where a fire breaks out in a crowded room. Everyone freezes in fear. One woman steps forward, directing people toward safety, grabbing an extinguisher, and calling 9-1-1. Her actions save lives, but equally important is how her calm tone comforts others and instills confidence.

The same principle applies at home: in moments of chaos, children draw emotional cues from us. When I was a child, my father revealed his calmness in a crisis. In 1976, we experienced the Tangshan earthquake, one of the deadliest earthquakes of the twentieth century. Waking up to loud noise and violent shaking, I could not move out of my bed. I started crying. Then, my father's hands reached for me. He lifted me up and carried me out of my bed. His tranquil voice soothed me, "There, there. We will soon get out of here. Don't be afraid—Dad is here with you."

That was just one of countless times he comforted me. When I failed an important exam, missed my driver's license test, lost my immigration papers, and struggled with my health, his calm demeanor reassured me, letting me know none of this was a big deal and that there was always a solution. His example taught me that serenity in crisis helps you find your way through dark moments.

As parents, here's what you need to understand and pay attention to:

1. Regulate your own emotions.

Children watch more than they listen. If we react to stress with anger, panic, or negativity, they will absorb and often mirror it. But if we take a breath, think, and respond with steadiness, they may also follow that example. Self-regulation isn't about never feeling upset; it's about pausing before we speak or act, and choosing a response that helps rather than harms.

2. Understand your child's emotional regulation.

One parent described to me that his daughter was such a drama queen. Her emotional rollercoaster changed day by day and hour by hour. "Why are teenagers so

crazy? One minute up, the next minute down?" There
are several reasons, including that adolescent brains
are not fully developed. The prefrontal cortex
(responsible for decision-making and impulse control) is
still developing, while the amygdala (emotional center)
is highly active. Another reason is that they are
experiencing hormonal changes.

Other reasons can be related to their own identity and
self-image and social pressures. For example, when
YouTubers show off their flat abs and ultra-thin bodies,
teens with slightly fuller figures may feel insecure or
ashamed; when celebrities post pictures with limited-
edition designer purses, some girls might question their
own families, especially those who live modestly. When
peers invite friends to concerts with hundred-dollar
tickets, teens who cannot afford to go may feel left out.
The list can go on and on and these may trigger
emotions. In moments like these, parents need to
remind their children that they are valuable, loved, and
worthy, regardless of what others have or show online.
As I often tell my children, "Underneath all the skin, we
are all the same." This is a reminder that external
appearance matters far less than inner character and
heart. It's the heart that truly matters.

3. Support your child's EQ growth

The question is whether our children can improve their
emotional intelligence. The answer is yes. While IQ

depends on many variables like environment and education, both of which can vary widely, EQ can improve through training, coaching, and practice.

That leads to the next question: How do we help them manage their emotions and improve their EQ? We can help them establish healthy habits while correcting self-image.

Another vital part of EQ is learning to form and sustain healthy relationships. Encourage your child to connect with others through shared activities, team projects, and acts of kindness. Teach them to listen actively, respect differences, and resolve conflicts without hostility. These skills prepare them to collaborate effectively — not only in school but in their future workplace and communities.

You Are A Vessel, I Am Your Master

Using the metaphor of 大器晚成 ("A great vessel takes time to be made."), remember that in order for a vessel to be made, many factors such as the clay, temperature, humidity, air, and pressure are involved. Success begins with sociability, that is, teaching children to learn they are not the only beings in their immediate world. To learn that because the world operates on a give-and-take basis, they must learn to cooperate with others.

When I was in elementary school, our teacher assigned a group arts and crafts project to be made out of paper. Every group wanted to be the best and first to finish because our grades would be based on speed and craftsmanship. In my group, I wanted to rush ahead, but my teammates insisted on spending time on the details to make it look beautiful. I grew impatient. I rushed, made mistakes, and then I pointed at others instead of fixing my problems: "Look at you! You messed it up."

Our teacher stopped what she was doing and looked at me. "You, you, you," she said. "All I hear is you blaming others. Is that really true?"

Her words hit me hard. Embarrassed, my face turned red. I cannot remember whether we won or not, but I remember my finger-pointing. From that day on, I learned to pause before criticizing others. As a result, I made more friends, with other kids growing more willing to play with me.

Years later, I am grateful for that moment. It taught me that success depends on teamwork and that blaming others only makes things worse. The older I get, the more I realize that maintaining harmonious relationships is not just beneficial but essential. Consider Academy Awards winners who acknowledge the contribution of their team and staff members in their award acceptance speech because they know that none of them achieved greatness without the help and trust of others. That's why I appreciate my teacher's words, despite her harshness. Learning to collaborate with others is an important skill in life, whether it's at home or work.

While parents, teachers and coaches can guide cooperation and collaboration, parents are the most influential figures in children's lives, especially in those formative early years. By modeling cooperation and respect, we can shape a vessel that is not only knowledgeable, but also has the ability to grow with others.

We have a Chinese saying, "榜样的力量是无穷的," meaning "The power of a role model is unlimited". It's not what you say; it's about what you do.

If you erupt in anger over small mistakes, but you want your child to keep calm, your child will not listen.

If you get stressed out over a minor mishap or accident but you want your child to keep calm, your child will not listen.

If you yell at other drivers on the road, and you want your child to forgive others, your child will not listen.

If you spend hours scrolling on your phone, and you want your child to spend less time on social media, your child will not listen to you.

You cannot change others forcibly, but you can influence them through your actions.

"Show, do not just tell." It does not matter how much you tell but what you do. So begin by taking your own advice according to that age-old adage, "Practice what you preach." In addition, you want to tell using your kind and warm words. "Show, and Tell"

My parents have always been my role models in parenting. My mother, in particular, was known for her kindness. Friends often told me how warmly she treated them and how generous she was toward others.

Her compassion came, in part, from her own life story. She grew up as an orphan because she lost both parents during World War II, and hardship taught her an important lesson: to survive difficult times, you must rely on others and be someone others can rely on. She carried that spirit of warmth and cooperation into her career.

In the 1970s, she worked at a research institute for metals and steel, leading the implementation of the institute's first electron microscope. It was a groundbreaking project that required strong project management, collaboration, and delegation. The challenges were many, but one stood out: the language barrier. The machine parts were imported from England, and all the instructions were in English. At that time, few people in China knew English, and of course, there was no internet to help. My mother taught herself the language, studying on her own, relying on dictionaries, doing research, and consulting anyone who could help.

Through persistence and teamwork, the project was completed on time. Her leadership kept the team motivated, her warmth kept relationships strong, and her contribution was instrumental to the project's success. I grew up hearing these stories from my parents. Their example of hard work and kindness helped shape the person who I am today.

Similarly, you should create time for your children by maintaining a strong relationship with them. Doing so will make it easier for you to teach and bond with them.

When our children reach elementary school, it's relatively easy to maintain good family dynamics compared to their toddler years. By then, they've acquired some self-control and can distinguish right from wrong. When they grow older, however, they become increasingly influenced by their peers, teachers, and perhaps the materials they learn in class essentially as the time they spend with their parents shrinks; this is all the more true when both parents work.

According to USAFacts, in the United States today, roughly three-quarters of mothers (73%) participate in the labor force (USAFacts team 2023). 81 percent of employed mothers with children ages 6 to 17 worked full time (Bureau of Labor Statistics News Release 2025). Parents who work full time generally only see their children from 6-10 pm—that is, when their sports, extracurricular activities or work commitments do not get in the way. Their children might spend their entire time studying in their own room, or chatting on social media with their friends.

When my children entered high school, we rarely had time together. Those brief twenty minutes at dinner did not provide sufficient time for mother-daughter chats, nor did the drive to their activities offer an ideal setting for in-depth discussion.

I wanted to rectify this situation. But how?

One of my friends suggested a simple method that required more effort than she expected. Nonetheless, it worked out. Deciding to create opportunities to be with her daughter and the latter's friends, she offered to drive them to their outings. She understood that being involved was the key.

My friend also went out of her way to find common interests with her daughter so they could hang out together at their favorite sports, concerts, and movies. Sometimes they cooked dinner or prepared brunch together. She realized that parents don't need to wait for their children to ask. Instead, they need to intentionally create opportunities for togetherness.

Similarly, find time for one-to-one time and family get-togethers. Private moments allow both parents and children to share their thoughts and feelings more openly, without judgment or interruption. As a mom of three, I learned the importance of having time to hear my daughters' thoughts and concerns. Sometimes, it was during a quiet drive home from her school events; at other times, it was a chat when we baked cookies and brownies together. My children grew to enjoy baking for their Bake for Charity Club, a club my two older daughters founded at their high school with the mission of baking and selling baked goods for charities.

The kitchen became more than a place for desserts: it became a safe place for conversation. While they whisked batter or decorated cookies, they often shared what was on their minds, with each other and with me. Since I was not nearly as skilled a baker as my daughters, I took on the duty of washing bowls and cleaning the counters. Interestingly, they tended to bake more often when they were stressed by schoolwork. For me, those baking sessions were the perfect chance to be their loyal listener.

Let's also not forget that when members of the family are away, family time together serves as a safe harbor. Ever since the pandemic, as my children attended colleges all across the country, family prayer on Sunday evenings via FaceTime became a critical time for us to support each other.

Nor should we overlook the importance of helping our children build good relationships with their friends. Even though I hosted birthday parties for them and invited their friends over for play dates, I nonetheless felt somewhat guilty about not doing more to create environments where friendships could grow. I thought children naturally made friends on their own. I paid even less attention when they became teens.

I also learned from another friend who hosted monthly BBQ parties at her backyard for her daughter and friends, which they thoroughly enjoyed. There were three considerable benefits. First, her daughter was able to invite her friends to her home, a safe place. Secondly, she eventually met all of her daughter's friends and listened to the newest and trending thoughts. And finally, her friends thought she and her mom were cool people.

The fact is the more time you spend on your relationship with your children, the stronger this relationship will be.

With Green Hills Standing, Firewood Won't Run Out (Healthy Habits)

Humans are creatures of habit. We tend to run on autopilot, following routines. We get up in the morning, prepare and eat breakfast, go to the office and return home after work. Then we make dinner, clean up, and go to bed. Our kids follow their routines too, going to school, hanging out with friends, engaging in sports or hobbies before returning home for dinner, completing homework, browsing the internet or social media, and going to bed.

As parents, we want to set up healthy routines.

1. To build healthy bodies, shop for healthy food and snacks. The importance of eating vegetables and fruits cannot be emphasized often enough. If your children want sweets, encourage them to eat fruit rather than processed snacks like cookies or cakes.
2. Create joy around meal preparation. Since cooking is such a fundamental skill, encourage your children to help out in the kitchen, especially when you're making their favorite dishes. Learning to cook helps them in multiple

ways, such as understanding nutrients, appreciating nature, and enhancing creativity. Moreover, this opportunity not only helps them learn the basics of cooking, but gives you time to chat and build stronger bonds with them.

3. Go to sleep early. Sleep deprivation is a pandemic around the world—especially since sleep can be far more important than food. Lack of sleep has negative impacts not only on physical growth but mental as well. I have a habit of sleeping early, usually around 10-10:30pm. Why not discuss it with your child and make it a priority?

4. Set up a time for exercise because it's part of a healthy lifestyle. Even fifteen minutes of yoga or stretching or tai chi can help anyone for the long run. Your child does not need to be sporty or join a sports club to be active.

Mirror, Mirror on the Wall, Who's the Fairest of All (Self-image and Self-identity)

Self-image is a factor that can have a significant impact on children. If we feel ashamed of ourselves or not good enough, we can feel nervous around others and wind up avoiding social interactions. Because of changing hormones and growth, teenagers often face anxiety about their self-image. This anxiety can be intensified by peers, who can be quick to judge, label, or call names. In the age of social media, rumors spread fast, adding pressure to fit in, look a certain way, or act according to group norms.

For instance, a friend's daughter felt self-conscious about her ears. Even though her ears were not overly large, she felt awkward when another girl called her "Monkey," especially as others followed her lead. Whenever taking pictures, she would use her hair to hide her ears. Years later, she still feels embarrassed about her ears.

Peer pressure can thus instill doubt in confident teens and even more so in those who already doubt themselves. They can fear public speaking, organizing an event, or taking on leadership roles. We, as parents, need to help them see themselves as more than adequate.

At the same time, excessively processed and filtered images can trigger anxieties in teens about their own images and identities. When they see manipulated images of tall, slim, and long-legged women or handsome men with perfect abs, they may wonder "Why can't I be like that?" They may try dangerous means of losing weight. And perhaps even worse, they may suffer hopelessness, body dysmorphia, and depression. Giulia Fioravanti and others have observed that viewing images on social networking sites depicting unattainable beauty ideals (i.e., thin, attractive, and fit) has a negative effect on body image, which is particularly problematic for adolescents who are still figuring out how they see and feel about their bodies (Fioravanti, et al. 2022). This becomes a barrier between teens and parents because teens often feel misunderstood or being judged if they share these insecurities. Many parents may dismiss these concerns as "not real life."

We need to praise the uniqueness of each child. I like the game that my daughter's 3rd grade teacher created for them. She had the children spell their names and use each letter to come up with a good word or a quality they admire in themselves. For example, Amanda might look like this:

> A - Adventure
> M - Mindful
> A - Authentic
> N - Nurturing
> D - Determined
> A - Ambitious

When children see their names associated with positive qualities, they gain confidence and feel proud of themselves. My youngest daughter's name starts with the letter "M". When I called her my "Magnificent" daughter, her face lit up. Her Chinese name contains a character 蜜, meaning honey. Whenever I called her the sweetest girl in the world, telling her she's as sweet as honey, she would give me a big smile.

Another good exercise is to teach children the "Mountain Pose," which involves standing tall and strong. As a child, I used to sit and stand with a hunched back until my father suggested the mountain pose, explaining that it would help me not only increase my intake of air but also make me look more confident. People often said my father had a "general's charisma" and "warrior's vibe" (大将风度).

He believed that posture doesn't just reveal inner strength but magnifies it. He simply knew that showing up each day with strength in your stance shapes how the world sees you—and how you see yourself. In fact, science has confirmed his intuition: standing tall can raise testosterone levels and boost confidence (Carney et al., 2010).

When performing this exercise, encourage your children to imagine they are a mountain—unshakable, strong, and dependable. Demonstrate it by standing firmly with your feet planted together, back straight, and shoulders rolled back.

We also need to discuss self-identity issues with your children. As immigrants to the U.S., we've all heard of the "Melting Pot" where people from different backgrounds, ethnicities, and religions join and live together in society. Prior to arriving in the US thirty years ago, the subject of discrimination and stereotypes never crossed my mind since I belonged to the Han majority in China. We looked the same, dressed the same, and mostly ate the same food. But in the US, I suddenly became a minority.

Several years ago, our company organized a workshop about diversity and inclusion. The facilitator asked each one of us to list our identity. In my list, I wrote, "I am Chinese. I am a mother. I am a Christian…" Then, I realized that I put my ethnicity at the top of the list. I suppose this is because I've always been aware of being a foreigner even though I have been in this country for thirty years, an immigrant who happens to be a Chinese woman.

When I had my children, I assumed they would be fortunate because they would not have culture and language barriers like me. But I soon learned that they were growing up under a different set of pressures.

"Emily said my face is flat." One day my daughter told me that. She didn't understand what that meant. How could someone have a flat face? The comment had a deeper meaning—Asian facial features have relatively little contrast in depth. Even though her friend did not necessarily intend to hurt her feelings, my daughter began to feel unattractive.

"White is the default." My Asian friend's daughter told her mom. That's probably coming from the perception from popular heroes on TVs or movies. The prevailing beauty standard still features Western faces. She felt invisible, convinced she could never be considered "popular" at school simply because she looked different. For a young girl still forming her self-image, the unspoken message was that no matter how kind, smart, or talented she was, she believed she would always fall short of Eurocentric standards of beauty.

There are other kinds of pressure too—the stereotype of the "model minority." My friend's son once said, "I got an A in math, but my friends told me it's only because I'm Chinese." What sounded like a compliment was actually a way of dismissing his hard work and reducing him to a racial caricature.

We need to be aware of cultural pressures that our children experience and discuss them openly. I like my friend's approach. A wise mother and devoted Christian, she knew that it was not easy to convince her children that they were beautiful and talented. So, she prayed aloud for them constantly, allowing them to hear her.

"Dear Heavenly Father, thank you for creating my beautiful children. They are created in your image. They are lovely children as all other children, white, black, and brown. Thank you for your love."

I also told my children that underneath their skin, you are the same as other children. Beauty standards change all the time. In the 18th and 19th centuries, European women with small waists were considered beautiful. In China, fat women were considered pretty in the Tang Dynasty, 618 - 907 AD (Ancient & Oriental 2025). Nowadays, thin women are considered attractive. Therefore, chasing after beauty standards is meaningless.

Last but not least, we need to take pride in our ethnic cultures. For my family, that means pride in being Chinese.

Since "white is the default" as my friend's daughter put it, it is all too easy for Asian children to struggle with their identity. What does being Asian or Chinese mean to them? While people harbor stereotypes about us, I like to think we not only have numerous assets, but that we need to instill pride in our Chinese heritage.

China has one of the oldest civilizations in the world, with thousands of years of philosophy, literature, and art. It continues to shape how people live today. Confucianism teaches respect, harmony, and responsibility; Daoism focuses on balance and humility. Together, they offer a deep well of wisdom that has been guiding people through hardship and change.

I like to share this wisdom with my children through stories and idioms. For example:

-   物极必反 (Extreme conditions lead to their opposites). This Daoist Concept reminds us that nothing stays one way forever. When life feels overwhelming, change is already on the way by natural force. It gives us a message of balance and hope.

-   饮水思源 (When drinking water, remember its source). This teaches gratitude—you should never forget those who came before us and made our life better. I tell my children this when I talk about my grandfather who joined the army to fight the Japanese and died on the battlefield during World War II.

-   宠辱不惊，闲看庭前花开花落 (Unmoved by honor or disgrace, I calmly watch the flowers bloom and wither before my courtyard). This teaches that we all have inner power to keep tranquility and content—not letting praise inflate you or criticism crush you.

Chinese culture also celebrates perseverance through vivid metaphors:

-   磨杵成针 (Grinding an iron rod into a needle). Even the impossible can be achieved with patience. If you can make a needle by grinding an iron rod, then you can achieve a lot by doing it persistently.

- 闻鸡起舞 (Rise at the crow of a rooster and start practicing). Discipline and diligence creates greatness. If you rise up as early as a rooster and start practicing, you may master a skill eventually.

- 百步穿杨 (Shooting a willow leaf from a hundred paces away). True skill comes from relentless practice.

When people hear these idioms, they tend to dismiss them as stale proverbs.

However, I want my children to view them as living lessons which apply to daily life. They are proof that our culture carries timeless wisdom regarding resilience, gratitude, and balance. These teachings are simple, direct, and wise, revealing cultural confidence and wisdom.

I also remind my children that our Chinese heritage is not only philosophical but practical. Traditional Chinese medicine has been practiced for thousands of years, saved countless lives, and much of its wisdom still proves true today. It is built on the idea of balance and harmony between the body, mind, and environment.

For example, I've learned over the years that drinking warm water helps calm the stomach and digestive system. Or take the practice of a foot massage: what began as a simple household remedy for circulation is now embraced around the world as "reflexology." Likewise, the custom of taking short daily naps is now supported by research showing it restores energy and sharpens focus.

Being Chinese is nothing to hide or downplay. It is a source of pride, a foundation that can strengthen their sense of self. Because when children know their roots, they stand taller.

We need to constantly remind our children that they are precious in their own ways. We need to teach them how they perceive themselves and show up in front of people. As they grow up, they will face challenges such as "model minority" and "bamboo ceiling." Knowing their identity will set up a solid foundation for future difficulties. If a teen complains about discrimination, parents need to step in with clarity and encouragement. We need to validate their frustration and remind them that Chinese culture has always valued perseverance, discipline, and hard work and these will help them build resilience and succeed in life. We also need to remind them of progress made in American society through the acknowledgment of discrimination and efforts to fight it over the last two centuries. Let them know their stamina is not for external approval, but for their own growth and choices.

Tony Robbins, a prominent coach and motivational speaker, said, "Identity drives your thoughts, decisions, and actions." Identity is the most powerful force in the human personality (Robbins 2025).

If you believe you are a loser, you will lose. If you believe you are a procrastinator, you will procrastinate. If you believe you are a failure, you will fail. On the other hand, if you believe you are a winner, you will win. If you believe you are an achiever, you will achieve. If you believe you are a warrior, you will fight fiercely. We need to teach our children to believe in themselves as someone outstanding and they will be outstanding.

Exercises

1. For one week, focus on maintaining calmness and patience in everyday interactions with your child.
2. Write a letter to your child, expressing your appreciation for him/her.
3. Each day, give one genuine compliment about their effort, kindness, or creativity.
4. Invite your child's friends to write one good trait about your child.

5. Do the name exercise as in the chapter (spell
    their names and use the first letter to come up
    with a good word.)
6. Ask your child to name a hero or celebrity of the
    same ethnicity.
7. Remind your child to stand tall and firm.

Chapter 8

Principle 5: Mend the Fence

"The only way to repair the world is to repair our relationships."
— NAOMI WOLF

When we say "亡羊补牢, 为时未晚" in Chinese, we mean, "Mend the fence when losing sheep; it's not too late." The phrase comes from *The Strategies of the Warring States*, an ancient text dating back over 2,000 years. The story tells of a man who lost his sheep from wolves because of a hole in the fence. His neighbor advised him to fix the fence, but he did not listen because he thought it was too late. The next day, another sheep disappeared. Finally, he repaired the fence and after that, the rest of his flock was safe.

The point is that if a fence breaks and you leave it unattended, the gap will only grow wider and allow more losses to occur. However, if you repair it in time, you restore both its strength and purpose so you will not lose more sheep (or sleep).

Although we are parents, we are still humans who make mistakes. We say mean things to our children when we lose our temper. Things can go wrong. What would happen if we did the same thing to our colleagues or friends?

I'm Sorry I Hurt Your Feelings (Apology)

We apologize and make up. A simple sentence like, "I'm sorry I hurt your feelings," usually removes all bad feelings and barriers.

But when facing our children, we are reluctant to admit wrongdoing—I am no exception. That's because we not only assume too much parental authority, but also because we feel we have done more than enough for them. We feel that we are older with much more life experience. It is the same reason that we don't feel we need to praise them too often. Sometimes, this refusal to apologize can turn into a "cold war," as we hold onto our grudges and refuse to speak or even acknowledge our children. Needless to say, such wars that last for days will only add stress for everyone in the family.

Over the years, I have learned to apologize to my children whenever I realize I've made a mistake, which has definitely helped improve our relationship. Here are a few ways to mend the situation before it is too late:

1. Apologize to them right away, directly looking them in the eyes.
2. If you feel uncomfortable with apologizing verbally, write a short letter.
3. Admit that you are imperfect, just like any human being.
4. Give them a warm hug and tell them you love them.

Take a Deep Breath (Stress Management)

As parents, we are bound to feel strained or exhausted after an argument or conflict with our children. One important factor is stress—whether ours or our children's. When under stress, our body generates adrenaline for survival. This may trigger poor judgment as our heartbeats quicken, all while we lose breath and unleash more arguments and conflicts. Before we know it, the argument turns into a screaming match where time is wasted and feelings are hurt.

This is why it's important to reduce stress before it gets out of hand. Stress management is a highly effective way of "mending the fence" and involves both managing your own stress and teaching your child how to manage it too. By doing so, we can also help our children build resilience and strengthen relationships with others.

1.   Give Mental Support

While apologizing is an important step, we also need to support our children emotionally when they struggle with mental stress.

"Mom, I'm hurt. I fell and sprained my ankle!" Your daughter calls for your attention after returning home from school. What would you do? Without thinking, you would probably jump up and rush to help her—checking on her ankle, leading her to the sofa, and asking her what happened. You would probably hug her and hand her a favorite fruit or drink. You would give whatever help she needs—at least that's what I did.

That's easy enough!

However, if she comes home, saying, "Mom, I'm sad. I got an F and my teacher's look said it all. I feel so stupid." What would you do? Hopefully, you will not do what I did, which was express disappointment before scolding her, saying, "An F? How did you do so poorly? Didn't you study last week?"

See the difference? My focus was not on her feelings, even though she appeared hurt and angry. My focus was on her grade and I expressed my disappointment by asking challenging questions.

As you can see, that was not a good way of showing support. Having already been distressed and angry at herself and her friends, she must have needed understanding and sympathy. Instead, I criticized her obliquely. Finding it difficult to answer my questions, she felt uncomfortable.

Why was it that I was able to respond correctly when my daughter sprained her ankle, but not when she felt anguished about her test? The difference was in my perception. A physical injury felt real and undeserved, so I reacted with care. But when she was hurting emotionally, I assumed it was her own fault that she got a poor grade and failed to see her pain. Parents need to give equal amounts of attention.

I wish I knew this years ago. What I did was add salt to the wound (伤口上撒盐). Remember the actions you took in the first case? Checking her ankle, leading her to the sofa, and asking her how she did it. You can do the same in this instance: discuss her hurt feelings, lead her to safety, and allow her to share her thoughts and feelings. Support for emotional pain is just as important as support for physical pain.

2. Reframe the Narratives

Another way to reduce stress is by shifting our perspective. Reframing narratives can help us and our children navigate challenges with less anxiety.

One of my favorite Taoist stories is 疑人偷斧, "suspecting others stole his axe." One day, a man lost his axe and immediately suspected that his neighbor's son had stolen it. As he watched the boy, every movement and expression seemed suspicious. His way of walking, his tone of voice, and even the way he looked at things all appeared guilty. The man was convinced that the boy was the thief.

Later, the man found his axe by chance. It had been misplaced in a spot he hadn't noticed. In other words, it was never stolen. The next day, when he saw the neighbor's son, the boy looked completely normal. His way of walking, his tone of voice, and even the way he looked at things all appeared ordinary. The suspicion had vanished, and the man realized that his judgment had been based on his own assumptions.

Have you ever experienced something similar? Once we believe something, confirmation bias kicks in as our imagination, wishes, or fears shape our perception for better or for worse. When we suspect our colleagues are badmouthing us, they suddenly appear sneaky and dishonest. And all too often, we stress ourselves out over our prefabricated narratives, sometimes even worrying about things that simply cannot happen or have a low probability of occurring.

Our children are the same and arguably worse because their brains are still developing and their life experience is limited. Small worries can quickly loom into big fears. That's the source of the tension that troubles them and will eventually trouble you.

One stress management strategy is to reframe the narrative. Let's go back to the story of the axe. When our child suspects someone "stole the axe," what should we do to help them?

Here, you might ask questions like, "When was the last time you saw your axe?" "What other places have you searched?" "Our neighbor's son, are you 100% sure he stole your axe?" "What other possibilities are there?" "Why would he do that?"

Or suppose your son is worried about his suspicion of being badmouthed by a friend. You can say: "When did you hear that?" "Can you think of other reasons he looked so sneaky?" "What makes you think he would do that?"

 You may also want to teach them to talk to themselves in a positive way.

"I have studied enough. I will get a good score."

"I did well last time. And I will do so again."

"Even if the result turns out unsatisfactory, I have no regrets because I have tried my best."

"What could be the worst? Even if I fail the exam, it's a good opportunity for me to learn more."

"I didn't put in enough effort before, but what I can do now is keep studying without letting it stress me out."

"Being anxious about the exam will not help me. I will remain calm and try my best."

"I believe in myself. I'm confident that I will do well."

3. Cooking or Other Fun Activities

A friend of mine, Amy, shared her story of how cooking with her daughter, Lisa, soothes the latter's mental distress. Lisa was a kind and smart girl, but occasionally "too sensitive," in her own words. She was doing well in her studies until high school, but suddenly started to stress out over everything from report cards to friendship and clubs. Amy tried different ways to help her. One day, Amy invited Lisa to bake a cheesecake for an upcoming birthday party. Lisa spent the whole morning with her mixing the ingredients and washing the bowls and pans. They laughed and danced along to the music at the same time. The joyful mood lasted the entire day and extended for another two days. It seemed to relieve all of her anxieties, making her troubles less daunting. From that time on, Amy would invite Lisa to cook and bake together every day.

Sometimes, even ten minutes of working in the kitchen would light up Lisa's face.

4. Meditation and Visualization

I have learned to use meditation and visualization to achieve my goals: for example, completing my book, passing the taekwondo promotion test, and competing at the Toastmasters speech contest. Coaches at the professional level often teach athletes the technique of visualization while athletes have confirmed their performance improvement after visualization. During their training, athletes picture themselves stepping into their roles at the game, visualizing each pitch, each punch, each body movement towards their opponents so they can replicate their actions at the actual game.

Visualization thus serves as a practical means of reducing stress, training our minds to practice under relatively less pressure. As long as we feel like we have practiced enough, we automatically relax our bodies and the stress level is lowered.

For example, if your child is anxious about performing a piano recital in the upcoming month, you may guide them to take several steps.
- Close your eyes and take a deep breath, in and out.
- Contemplate the abdominal area while inhaling and exhaling slowly.

Now, imagine:

- Walking up to the stage and bowing.
- Walking to the piano with a smile on your face.
- Sitting down and putting your music sheet on the sheet frame.
- Your hand touching the piano keys, feeling confident and grounded.
- Playing from the first to the last note as you usually do at home.
- Your audience enjoys listening to the music.
- Finishing your piece strongly, with the audience applauding.
- Turning to the audience, giving them another big smile.
- Standing up and bowing to them, appreciating their applause.
- Calmly walking down the stage, with a winner's smile.

You may do this visualization exercise with your child at home, which will alleviate their anxiety and improve their actual performance. In the long term, your child will apply these techniques to other stressful situations.

May God Bless You, My Child (Bless Your Child)

In Chinese, there's a phrase, "心誠則靈，祝福成真." It means, "When the heart is sincere, it will be effective and blessings will come true." In our culture, we often wish others good health, plenty of fortune, career advancement, and happiness during the Lunar New Year or birthday. Many believe it is extremely important to express good wishes during the Lunar New Year period for fear that the good fortune will leave the house.

I did not believe this when I was little as I privately smiled at the elderly for their silly superstitions. I believed back then that blessings were just a polite way of showing gratitude and maintaining good relationships with others.

Since becoming a Christian, I often pray and send my blessings to others. I pray for my family and friends, believing that God has mercy on us and will help us fulfill our wishes. I knew God is powerful, but doubted the strength of human blessings relative to prayer. After all, we are only human and how could our words alone bring dreams to true? Many years ago, I doubted the power of our own words until a friend of mine, Anna, shared a story about her son, Tom.

Tom was a teenager, a smart kid, but strong-willed. One day, he refused to go to school and stayed in bed for the entire day. Anna was angry and naturally worried about his grades which had slipped so much over the semester. She tried to talk to him through the closed door as the boy locked himself up, refusing to talk to her.

Anna shouted, "If you don't go to school, how can you catch up in your class? Please remember that if you don't catch up, you will fail; if you fail your classes, you will fail school and not graduate…" She continued.

The second day, Tom finally went to school, but kept his distance from Anna.

He lagged behind on his homework. Once again, he refused to go to school for a few days and locked himself up. Anna was furious because the semester would end soon, so she banged on the door, shouted her lungs out, venting her anger. Nothing worked. He only came out of his shell when he was hungry.

Not surprisingly, several F's appeared on his transcript. Desperate, sad, and heartbroken, Anna spent her whole day thinking about how miserable life was. She tried to be a loving mother—cooking, cleaning, buying nice clothes for him, yet he did not even want to talk to her. What went wrong?

Anna slowed down and meditated on the whole thing. She finally realized that the very fears she had voiced about failing school had come true. While her husband was often away on business trips, she carried the responsibility of caring for her son alone, and the weight all left her feeling suffocated. Around that time, she read about a Jewish tradition which encouraged parents to bless rather than curse their children. The overall principle is that we should send good wishes and blessings to our children so they can flourish like healthy crops. On the other hand, when you convey worries to your children, they will wind up becoming just what you worry about. In short, the book taught her to reframe her negative thoughts into positive wishes, even in the worst circumstances.

Anna decided to give it a try. She stopped yelling and screaming at her son from that day on. Instead, she started visualizing her boy going back to school, doing well, and passing all of his classes. She also wished her son well while silently verbalizing these wishes to herself, "May he get up and go to school. May he be well. May he enjoy school. May he thrive academically. May he make good friends. May he feel good about himself. May he feel love." Then, she felt comforted and relaxed.

After a few days, Tom went back to school—probably curious about his mother's sudden change. The mother was the same, still doing the same chores. The only difference was that she smiled at him, wishing him a nice day every morning. Sometimes, she added a few more wishes such as, "May you do well in your tennis competition," "May you have fun swimming," or "May you get help in your algebra class."

He was surprised to see a calm mother who didn't criticize. A couple of months later, near the end of the semester, she too was surprised—the boy not only caught up with his classmates, but also won a math competition. She was proud of her son and equally proud of herself for realizing the necessity of change.

"You need to put all of your wishes and blessings for your children into words." Anna shared with me, smiling. "Then your wish will be fulfilled."

"Really? Everything?" I hesitated.

"For parenting, yes. I started giving blessings to other things, such as my health, my relationship with my husband… And so far it works perfectly for me." She paused before answering.

I could not believe Anna entirely at that time. Several years later, when I struggled with my children, I thought about her advice and discovered it worked. As she suggested, words are powerful and harbor energy. When we speak out wishes for our children, we convince our hearts that they will have a bright future. Our calmness is contagious and guides our children in a positive way. It tells them that Mom believes that they will be able to handle challenges in school.

As for Tom, he must have experienced difficulties at school, either with a teacher or his friends. Or perhaps he simply tired of a busy school schedule, feeling pressured. Whatever the reason, he felt unhappy and inadequate. His mother's kind wishes instilled a belief in his improvement which in turn boosted his own self confidence. He eventually opened up to her, shared his struggles in friendship, and appreciated his mother's patience and love.

If you want happy children, you need to become a happy mom. If you believe in your children, they will believe in themselves. If you keep a positive attitude during difficult times, your child will use positivity to overcome difficulties, because ultimately, they learn from you.

My Child is Mentally Ill (Seek Professional Help)

Mental disease is one of the top causes of damaged well-being and ruined relationships. There are many factors contributing to anxiety, depression, or other forms of mental disease. Parents may or may not directly cause the children's instability, or even worse, parents themselves may struggle because of their own pressures from work, relationships, and so on. In the case that parents themselves are not mentally healthy, children might be impacted even more negatively. When both parents and children suffer mental health issues and parents, their relationship can fray badly.

It's worth bringing up mental health, especially for immigrants. The word "mental health" was a very new concept for me and other Asian parents. It certainly felt very foreign to me when I was in my twenties, partly because no one around me seemed to discuss such issues, especially since no mental health offices existed on campus.

But then I recalled that many of my friends experienced anxiety or depression at times. And so did I. We all encountered academic stress, relationship crises, friendship dramas—which we all acknowledged as part of life. However, we never really thought about any other solution other than treating ourselves to a good meal, wandering about the campus, crying on friends' shoulders, or journaling endlessly. So we were fine, growing from teenagers to adults to becoming parents. "What mental health? It's for crazy people who suffered traumas and abuse. Not for us," many of us thought.

We are not alone in this belief. Many Generation X people grew up in an era when mental health was rarely discussed (Baral et al. 2022). Several decades ago, the general concept of mental health took a backseat to other issues, such as drug addiction, alcoholism, gun violence, and so on. But over the years, a growing number of people have begun to discuss mental health as diagnoses have risen sharply and its marked impact on overall well-being became impossible to ignore. According to a recent survey, an overwhelming majority of people in the United States think the country is experiencing a mental health crisis with major concerns around youth mental health, severe adult illness, and the opioid epidemic. (McPhillips, 2022). Mental health has become an important component as part of overall health and wellbeing, with many realizing that physical and mental health are inseparable (Ring, 2021). A fully functioning human needs to have a healthy body and mind.

My understanding of mental health has evolved so much as well after observing many cases within my circle of friends, including adults and adolescents.

First, I accepted the fact that everyone can have a mental breakdown at sometime in life. No one can ensure that they are totally immune.

Second, it's treatable and needs our attention, just like any other health issue in the body.

Third, we need to support each other and seek professional help when needed.

Another buzz word I have often heard is PTSD, or post trauma stress disorder. It's a condition that can develop after experiencing a traumatic event, be it abuse, war, accident, etc. Some people were knocked down while others not only survived, but also showed up stronger. If we can learn from those who became stronger, we can certainly help ourselves and others around us do the same to build resilience.

As an Asian American, I have observed that the Asian community tends to refrain from seeking professional help when facing mental health issues. A related study found that white US citizens take advantage of mental health services at three times the rate of Asian Americans (Nishi, 2012). Asian Americans do not feel comfortable talking about psychological disorders, feeling shame and embarrassment. It is important to raise awareness of needing help from others, including mental health professionals, as a way of demonstrating strength, rather than the opposite.

There are two ways or levels of help you may consider:

1. Counselors and Coaches

Teachers and counselors are the first level of resource you may seek help with. They have first-hand information about your child. They understand the complexity of the social dynamics, academic requirements, and school district system.

I would suggest all parents connect with their child's teachers. If there's a particular issue, they can jump in and help. For example, if your child complains about bullies, you might communicate it to the teacher.

Each school district has licensed mental health professionals who have experience in working with children while many schools have onsite mental health offices. The office usually requires appointments to be made ahead of time, but also accepts walk-ins. It's free, convenient, and friendly as my children, along with their friends, have discovered.

Outside of school, parents may find coaches or mentors for their children which can be helpful since some children pay more attention to those outside of their family. There are plenty of successful stories out there. For example, Adventures in Wisdom reported a successful life coach, Tom Kuestner who dedicated himself to teaching swimming to children and teens, serving as a camp counselor, and coaching various youth sports teams (Robertson 2023). As a teacher, he coached kids for mindset skills training at the side. His coaching positively impacted many young lives, including members of a basketball team and a young swimmer dealing with anxiety.

2. Medical Professionals

Seeking help from medical professionals is necessary when you feel that a situation is spinning out of control. Even if you think you are beginning to find a disturbing pattern of behavior, it's still good to get a consultation at an early stage. It shows that you pay attention to your child's needs and you are willing to make every effort to

help your child. It opens a door for the child to find
support and solace.

Among my friends, many have sent their children to see
a therapist. Initially, no one wanted to discuss it out of
shame, but eventually someone started asking around
for recommendations. Once one parent opened up that
her child is seeing a therapist, other parents slowly
admitted that their children were also seeing one too.

One parent even says, "Seeing a therapist is so
common now. It's like braces, a sign of maturity and
almost every kid needs to go through the correction
process in order to have perfect teeth."

Exercises

1. Write an apology letter if it's hard for you to
    apologize verbally to your child for your mistake.

2. When seeing your child upset, start with an
    empathetic statement like, "I see that you're feeling
    really upset. Tell me what happened."

3. Do the following exercise with your child together.
    a. Write down a stress-inducing thought.
    b. Rewrite it with a positive reframe.
    c. Teach your child how to do this exercise for
        their own challenges.

4. Guide your child through a visualization exercise before his/her sports competition or test.

5. Practice meditation with your child.

6. Cook or bake with your child.

7. Discuss with your child that seeking help is a sign of strength, not weakness.

PART 3

RISE FOR YOURSELF

Chapter 9

Principle 6: Fill Your Cup First

"I love him so much. I'd die for my son. I'd do anything for him. But he will not listen to me; he will not talk to me; he does not like spending time with me. He's like a stranger. No love for me," a friend wiped her tears while telling me about his son.

I could feel her pain from her quivering lips. As a mom, of course, I also want my children to love me back.

But, what is love? If you ask a hundred parents, you will probably receive a hundred answers. For some, love means affection and closeness; for others, it means meeting a child's needs with food, shelter, and care;

and for still others, it means responsibility, effort, and respect.

When I attended the educational training for parents in 2014, "Communicate with Strong-Willed Adolescents," one of the first sessions focused on love: "Love 101." I thought, "Who would need this sort of lesson?"

The majority of the parents in the audience were in their thirties and forties with a few perhaps in their fifties, but all of us had difficulty communicating with our teenage children. We didn't think we needed to learn about loving our children. We poured out our hearts and souls to our children. We certainly loved them. We did not need anyone to question our love or teach us to love our children. But, do we know what love is—let alone unconditional love?

I started searching for answers. I gave birth to my children, nursed them, fed them, dressed them, sent them to school, played with them, kissed them, hugged them, and watched them grow each day. Wasn't this good enough?

I began to think perhaps it was good love, but not as unconditional as I thought it was.

We are tested when there's a conflict—when our children talk back to us; when they argue with us; when they roll their eyes at us; when they scream at us; when they throw things on the ground; when they look down on our lessons, even values.

Are we able to give them a hug telling them "I love you?" We all sighed. We may not be able to say, "I love you," at least at that moment.

During training sessions, we learned how brain development affects teenage emotions and behavior. For example, their prefrontal cortex—the part responsible for judgment, impulse control, and long-term thinking—is still maturing. Teens tend to react more emotionally. With this knowledge, we learned to communicate with them with empathy and patience. We also practiced new communication techniques with our children. For example, using open-ended questions, listening actively, etc. The core behind these actions is none other than unconditional love.

We all know "Love is patient; love is kind." But, how can we have patience and kindness when our rebellious children are screaming at us or refusing to talk? We sometimes joked that people should pass a certification test before having a child, one titled "Certified Parents."

The training sessions also taught us something we rarely talk about as parents: self-love. Unconditional love requires strength and that strength must come from somewhere. Before we can offer patience, grace, or kindness to our children, we must first learn to care for ourselves. Years later, those lessons continue to shape the way I parent and the way I nurture myself.

Leave Me Alone Please (Set Up Boundaries)

In her book, *Mama Needs a Refill*, Jenny McGlothern emphasizes the importance of self-care for caregivers, particularly mothers. She introduces the metaphor of the "cup" to represent one's soul and inner resources, explaining that one cannot pour from an empty cup (McGlothern 2023, 23). It entails the importance of setting boundaries for self-care and self-love.

When we discuss boundaries, we are inclined to think of work. We think about the number of projects on our plates, how much more we can take on, and when to push back and say "no." This is good advice for anyone at the workplace, especially as we observe more and more burnout in recent years. Two of my female friends were forced to visit the emergency room due to burnout at work within the past year.

However, setting up boundaries is equally important at home. Even when mothers work outside the home, they continue to do most of the chores around the house while supervising their children. A report from the Gender Equity Policy Institute (GEPI) shows that mothers typically spend about 12 hours per week taking care of children compared to 6.7 hours for fathers, meaning that mothers spend 2.3 times as much time (Barela and Moridi, 2024). Combining childcare and household work, mothers spend 2.1 times as much time as fathers on the essential and unpaid work of caring for the family. This disparity highlights why we need to carve out time for ourselves and protect our own well-being.

Setting up boundaries means letting other family members share responsibilities around the house. However, many Chinese mothers would rather assume all household responsibilities than delegate tasks to their spouses and children.

One reason for this habit is that they were raised this way—their mothers were also the ones to single-handedly complete every household task. Historically, Chinese men were not expected to do any chores. As women observed their mothers and grandmothers carrying on responsibilities, many felt guilty about letting their husbands or children—especially boys—help out at home. One mother told me, "I'm not teaching my son to cook. I will not let him be his wife's servant in the future." I was surprised by her claim, because women of my generation were open to the idea of having men take on equal responsibilities around the house.

Many Asian mothers also think no one else can do a better job. This preconception, which is sometimes subconscious, should be rejected. It's actually not unlike work—just as leaders need to learn to delegate projects to junior team members, mothers need to delegate house work to others. Delegation can actually help children develop life skills.

At the same time, some Chinese mothers feel that children need to spend more time on academics or activities that prepare them for college and a future career. Given today's highly competitive environment, they think, "Why not let the children develop other skills such as in computer programming, graphic design, or writing?" Housework, according to these mothers, is a waste of time. One mother told me when I suggested the benefits of teaching children to cook at an early age, "Children will eventually learn how to cook when they grow up. There is no need for them to do tedious kitchen work."

In order for mothers to fill their cups, they should allow their family members to share a few responsibilities around the house. These chores can teach children basic life skills and independence while releasing mothers from their burdens. Setting boundaries shows that you are as important as other family members and friends.

Take a Breath, Not the Bait (Discipline with Grace)

Beyond setting up boundaries, mothers also need to protect themselves from being hurt emotionally. Some mothers are too accommodating to their children, thinking they need to give into their child's every demand.

When their children throw tantrums, they rush to appease them. Later on, some of the same mothers feel manipulated and unappreciated. Mothers need to have clear rules, such as no shouting, no disrespectful language, no tantrums, etc.

One technique I learned over the years when dealing with arguments is to walk away silently. This technique can cool down tempers while signaling that the conversation has violated your boundaries and needs to be paused.

When the little one says something inappropriate that angers you, what's the best way to handle the situation? Here are the steps that I found useful:

First, take several deep breaths. This will calm your nerves, preventing any rash actions or shouting something you will regret later.

Second, look into your child's eyes and say, "I do not appreciate what you said." This clearly states that you do not tolerate this kind of behavior.

Third, say no more and walk away quietly. This deescalates the situation by ending the conversation.

Fourth, talk to them about the house rules, such as "no screaming, no yelling, no swearing" and explain the reasons when the child is willing to listen. If they don't follow the rules, I stay calm and simply remind them. Sometimes their behavior is caused by hunger, fatigue, or overstimulation, so I make sure their physical needs are met first. If the behavior continues, I gently distract them from whatever triggered the outburst. And if things escalate further, I provide space and let them release their energy. When they finally settle, I return to them with a calm reminder of the rule and the reason behind it.

One time, my 3-year-old daughter was angry about not seeing a book that she liked in a local library. She started screaming and crying in the quiet library. I reminded her to lower her voice and explained to her that the book would probably return next week. No matter what I tried, it didn't seem to work. I then cuddled her and distracted her attention to some other books. She finally fell asleep in my arms after being exhausted. My soothing manner apparently helped her to calm down.

I know it's easier said than done. I have learned from my own mistakes over the past twenty something years.

The whole process is to teach your child from an early age to model your behavior in the face of crisis. Your calm demeanor helps you find a solution through inner power; and they have the ability to do so too. When they grow up, they will appreciate you for being an outstanding example in handling tough situations. Self-love always comes first no matter what challenges we are faced with.

"Love is patient; love is kind" goes a long way. It starts with yourself. Only when you are full of love, which involves being patient and kind to yourself, do you have the capacity to be patient and kind to your child and others around you.

Let Me Eat First (Love Yourself)

You don't need to be capable of doing everything that a good mom is supposed to do.

Some believe there are moms who can handle every situation very smoothly—the ones who don't get mad at their children; are always smiling; keep their houses clean; cook the best meals; host parties for their children with smooth assurance; entertain them constantly; dress nicely and keep slim; act with confidence; succeed professionally; have good relationships with their colleagues and friends; take care of the house, husband, and children; earn a large salary; volunteer at their children's school. They seem to have it all.

Scratch that. Such a portrait can only be found in Hollywood—if at all.

I remember enjoying a *Desperate Housewives* episode where one character drew my attention. It was Lynette, who seemed like a smart, ambitious woman. She had a thriving career before choosing to stay home with her four children. But she had her own struggles as the show unfolded. Although she got frustrated with her children while her marriage fell apart, she wound up with a happy ending after so many heartbreaking moments. She managed to succeed at home and work, becoming a good mom.

I do not know any have-it-all moms in my circle, nor am I a "perfect" mom myself despite having friends praise me for succeeding in many aspects of life. I have had my own challenges, all while new ones turn up every day.

We all understand the importance of putting on our own oxygen mask before helping others with theirs during an airplane emergency. Similarly, in order to love others, we need to love ourselves first.

"Only when your cup is filled, can you pour it out to others. Love is the same thing. When our heart is full of love, we pour out our love towards others." One of my wise friends shared it with me many years ago.

Similarly, Jenny, one of my author friends, pointed out in her book *Mama Needs a Refill* that we need to constantly fill our cups before emptying. I was immediately drawn to the title of her book.

"Of course, everyone needs a refill." She told me, "Especially women, mothers!"

That totally resonated with me. If our cups are empty, how can we help others? Also, "love your neighbors as yourself" is a lesson from the Bible. People stress the first part of the sentence—"love your neighbors," but neglect the later part—"love yourself." If you treat yourself poorly, you will treat others poorly.

However, in Chinese culture, virtue involves putting others first and our own needs last. Women are particularly taught to be caring and to put their children first. Years ago, when resources were scarce, mothers often saved food for their children. There is no doubt that such actions demonstrate great love, reinforcing the notion that no love can exceed a mother's love. Today, our instinct still tells us to sacrifice even though resources may be more abundant. We give up sleep, energy, and time all too quickly to tend to our babies in early years. Yet, even as we care for them, we must remember not to lose ourselves entirely. And more importantly, we need to bear in mind that self-love is not selfish, but instead necessary for a healthy relationship with anyone—including our children.

When my children were infants, I would rush home from work to nurse them, often exhausted and hungry. My mother-in-law always had dinner ready (back then my in-laws stayed with us to take care of my children while I was at work). She would gently urge me to eat first, understanding how tired I was. But the sound of my crying baby made me hesitate. Sometimes I quickly inhaled my meal before nursing; at other times, I grabbed a snack with one hand while cradling the baby in the other. I genuinely appreciated my mother-in-law's assistance and understanding my inner voice of "Let me eat first."

That's why I always encourage the women around me to take care of their needs first. You will have the calmness, energy, and wisdom to help your children when you are recharged. Here's a list of simple things you can do to help yourself.
   1. Set up a space away from your child and family; even 30 minutes a day is helpful.
   2. Do something exciting for yourself, not your child.

3. Treat yourself a nice meal, nap, walk, or massage.
4. Meditate for 15 min.
5. Talk to a friend who knows you well.

There are other ways to improve your well-being, e.g. listening to music, gardening, exercise, and so on. Fill your cup with activities that you feel relaxed and pleasant. Do these because you want to do them, not because you do them for other people.

I Thank Myself for Being Amazing (Practice Gratitude Towards Yourself)

Many of us understand the importance of practicing gratitude because it helps us improve happiness. One thing I would like to point out is that we tend to show gratitude towards others, not ourselves.

If we are used to sending an appreciation letter or love letter to others, why can't we do the same for ourselves? In *Stepping Into Love,* Angela M. Smith asks us, "If I asked you to name all the things you love, how long would it take before you included yourself? (Smith 2023, 83)"

What an enlightening message!

Being grateful for yourself may sound strange, but it's the easiest way and best way to give yourself a well-deserved award.

I know a lot of people practice daily affirmations. I do too. I would say something like.
- "I am amazing."
- "I am talented."
- "I am beautiful."

It is one form of expressing gratitude. Over the years, I have added the following.
- "I have achieved so much."
- "I thank myself for working so hard."
- "I am proud of myself for being a good mom."

These reminders have helped me tremendously. Once I fill my own cup, I become more content and calm. All of the challenges I face have become solvable. The family dynamic has turned to more positive and harmonious. Like people say, "Happy mom, happy family."

Therefore, fill your cup first, so that you may have more to give to your child. Filling your own cup gives you the calmness your body and mind need. That's precious. And it's contagious - your child will feel it.

Exercises

1. Self-Love Reflection

Write down five things you love about yourself as a
parent, e.g. what you did well this week that had a
positive impact on your child.

2. The Self-Care Challenge

Choose one self-care activity from the list provided in
the chapter and commit to doing it for this week. Write
down how it makes you feel and whether it affects your
interactions with your child.

3. Setting Boundaries Exercise

Identify one area where you need to set a boundary
with your child (e.g., your own time and space,
disrespectful language, too many responsibilities on
your plate). Write down one specific step you will take
this week to reinforce that boundary.

4. Gratitude Letter to Yourself

Write a short letter to yourself expressing gratitude for
all that you do as a parent. Reflect on the challenges
you've faced and celebrate your wins. End the letter by
affirming your worth and resilience.

5. Reframing Expectations

Think of a recent situation where your child did not
meet your expectations. Use the self-talk suggestions
from the chapter to reframe the experience in a more
positive and accepting way. Write down how this shift
in perspective changes your feelings.

Chapter 10

Principle 7: Be the Hero You Want to See

"The only person you are destined to become is the person you decide to be."
— RALPH WALDO EMERSON

If we want our children to advance in their studies, we need to continue learning ourselves. If we want our children to exercise more, we need to be more active ourselves. If we want them to care more about society, we should lead by example through volunteering. In other words, we should be the hero that we wish our children to become.

Put Down Your Phone (Be a Life Long Learner Yourself)

When you remind your child not to spend too much time on their phones or social media, you need to put down your phone first. Remember, they learn from your example.

If you want your child to gain new knowledge, you need to keep learning yourself. "Stay foolish. Stay hungry," was popularized by Steve Jobs during his 2005 commencement address at Stanford University. It quickly became one of my favorite quotes. This quote, however, was actually created by Stewart Brand for the Whole Earth Catalog, a publication that offered tools and ideas to foster individual initiative and self-education. Jobs adopted this mantra to encourage continuous learning and a willingness to take risks. Similarly, the Chinese saying "如饥似渴" which translates to "As hungry as if starving, as thirsty as if parched" describes an intense eagerness or desire to learn, achieve, or acquire something—comparable to someone craving food when starving or water when dehydrated.

A friend of mine came to the U.S. when her son was in high school. The son struggled at school because of language barriers. Watching her son almost fail academically, becoming depressed, she decided to attend community college to learn English. It not only helped her improve her proficiency, but also turned her into a good role model for her son. After the first two difficult years, her son eventually graduated from the high school with good grades. She also received her AA degree from the community college. While her son

left home for college, my friend transferred her credits
to UC Berkeley. When he graduated from college four
years later, she had already graduated from UC
Berkeley and found a new job. She did not stop there,
but continued to pursue her MBA degree from an
online university. When I asked her how she could
achieve so much in multiple areas, she answered:

"First is the motivation. I initially just wanted to prove to
my son that his mother in 40s could learn. And that he
could learn as well. Secondly, the more I learn, the
more interested I become in the subjects I discovered
in the books. Knowledge is powerful," she continued.

She then smiled, pushing up her glasses a bit, "If you
ask me *how* I had time, I knew I could only do it by
cutting out all social media. I removed all my apps from
my phone, making my smartphone a dumb phone."

If you are hungry for knowledge, your child will follow.
Then, put your phone down and be a role model for
your child.

When I joined Toastmasters in 2009, my sole purpose
was to improve my communication and leadership
skills. I participated in the program, volunteering to
serve as a club officer before serving as a district officer.
Inspired by other toastmasters because of their passion
and devotion, I also inspired others—especially those

with a similar background, including immigrants and women.

I did not expect my children to be influenced by me. Later on, I invited them to volunteer at speech contests as I began organizing the Toastmasters Youth Leadership Program which included eight weeks of teaching and practicing. My children attended with their friends and had the opportunity to improve their speaking skills.

None of us can survive without our community. This is because our children need their support system, including parents, friends, teachers, mentors, and others. Toastmasters is a program that shows how parents can become highly involved for themselves and their children.

There are other programs out there where parents might lead their children. Some of my friends were highly involved in the baseball program or volunteered to be the soccer coach; some of them became soccer coaches. They were not that good at these sports at the beginning, but by leading the program they grew more themselves.

You don't need to know everything before starting a program. It's like writing a book. You don't need to know everything before you start writing. You write or teach while you research and learn yourself. In the process, you not only grow more skilled and experienced, but also build a community for your children.

You Are My Teacher, My Child (Learn from Your Child)

"How do I change the format in this Canva file?" I asked my oldest daughter on our Zoom call. "Mom, let me show you." She replied on the other side, sharing her screen. Yes—she's my teacher.

The coolest teachers ever are my children! Just a few years back, they asked me everything, and now I'm the one asking them everything. They've shown me that life's classroom is rich and vibrant, full of surprises that only they can unveil.

Lesson number one: Yoga. Life got crazier as I hit 45 a few years ago especially as my friends tossed around the term "Fifty Years Shoulder" which sounded absolutely terrifying to me. It was all about aches and pains creeping in.

Then one day, as I was telling my daughter about the "Fifty Years Shoulder," she told me excitedly, "Mom, yoga helped me relieve my back pain. You've got to try it." She then introduced me to Square One Yoga Studio. That's when I realized that yoga wasn't just stretching and balancing but was a mental and physical journey to connect with my inner self. Flexibility wasn't just about my body; it was about finding inner peace. Who knew? This journey into yoga has taught me the importance of balance, both in body and mind, and the significance of nurturing the connection between the two.

Moving on to the second lesson—Taekwondo. When my eldest started this journey ten years ago, I never thought I'd be kicking and punching with her. Year by year, she advanced from the white belt all the way to the junior black belt.

She invited me many times, "Would you join taekwondo?"

I declined because I never considered myself martial arts material. But when she wanted to quit taekwondo during her sophomore year in high school because of heavy school assignments and activities, I encouraged her to continue to get her black belt, saying, "Once you achieve your black belt, I'll start taekwondo." Her eyes sparkled. She continued till two years later when she achieved her black belt.

On the day celebrating her black belt, she invited me, "Mom, it's your turn to join me!" I was surprised, assuming that she had probably forgotten my promise from two years ago. So, I reluctantly joined taekwondo.

That was six years ago. Now, I'm at the black belt level I. Without my daughter's prodding, I would have never achieved this much.

The third lesson emerged with my children's appreciation of the arts. My background was STEM, and I never believed I would be interested in any form of art. But their love for painting, drawing, and even culinary art opened up a whole new world for me. They loved spending time in art museums wherever we traveled, whether it was Paris, London, or Barcelona. Similarly, I grew interested as my second daughter enjoyed adding artistic touches to her cooking when she made cookies, brownies, cakes, noodles, and pasta. Likewise, when she developed an interest in pottery, I started paying attention to bowls and plates. That may be why I found myself admiring the containers and vases as much as the flowers at the Dahlia Show. I like to think I would not have noticed as much artistry without my daughters.

As parents, we may often feel that we are the ones guiding our children, but in reality, they guide us too, lighting our way with their passion and unquenchable curiosity. We should embrace the lessons they teach us as we continue to improve while nurturing their dreams and celebrating their growth.

That's why I've come to believe my coolest teachers are my children. I know my children feel that I'm so incompetent in numerous areas, including technology, art, and language, but their shining eyes and nodding indicate that they are willing to show me and enjoy teaching me. From them, I learned how to "talk" to Siri on my iPhone and even ask her to set alarms for me. When they discover a new book or visit a new museum, they eagerly share their insights with me, always again to inspire me. They even keep me updated on trendy words, such as "low-key" or "LMAO" and these help me better understand their world. That's why I know that my children admire that I'm still willing to learn, always excited to be their most curious student.

Beyond all of the lessons they had given me, my children became my biggest cheerleaders when I decided to write my book. In the summer of 2022, I began that journey during the most difficult year of my life, just months after losing my father in January. Writing was a healing process. My children believed that I would be able to complete the book and make it beautifully written. I did it. I wrote my book and published it in November 2023.

Learning is a two way process—you can always learn from your child. Learning from your child shows not only your eagerness to learn but your humility too.

I'm Building a Village To Raise You (Build a Community)

Ideally, the community you build should also nurture your children while connecting them to other friends. Since friendship is extremely important during adolescence—perhaps just as important as their studies, we should aim to not only become our children's friends, but also help them develop friendships with those in their age group.

Church is another great community that benefitted my children. Although my older children went off to college a few years ago, they still kept in touch with their friends from church. When they came home during holidays, they would all get together. My guess is that they will become forever friends—friends who are like family, where bonds can be even thicker than blood.

Volunteering is yet another good way to build a community. Occasionally, I took our children along with their friends to volunteer at various places with the most frequent one being the Bay Area Rescue Mission where they enjoyed working in the kitchen, cutting vegetables, sorting breads, and mixing eggs. While volunteering and contributing to the shelter, they collaborated with their friends and caught up with each other in the classroom and news gossip.

Finally, you'll want your children to be surrounded by supportive people and have a sense of belonging: this is especially important if your child feels isolated because of their ethnicity or race—or wants to feel more connected to those with a similar background. This is—after all—how so many immigrants to the US, whether from Asia, or anywhere else helped piece their knowledge together as they learned.

For example, Albany API-PEG (Asian Pacific Islanders-Parent Engagement Group) has proven to be a supportive community for parents and students in Albany and its neighborhood. API-PEG was founded during the period of "Stop Asian Hate", where many violent acts were perpetrated against Asians after the Corona virus breakout in 2020. At the beginning, I only participated in the street rallies and demonstrations. I eventually took a leadership role, serving as a co-chair of the monthly Speakers Series, inviting experts to share their experiences and knowledge on Asian-American life. Later on, I took further action by becoming co-chair of the API-PEG. On behalf of the API, I spoke at the high school diversity week assembly, accepted the proclamation of Asian Heritage Month by the City of Albany and organized the Lunar New Year celebration. All of these events helped parents and children feel a sense of belonging as we celebrated our cultural heritage together.

Many immigrants may not feel comfortable volunteering at the API events or PTA events. One reason is that they feel that as newcomers, they do not understand the rules. Another is that they lack confidence about their linguistic abilities. However, I have seen many Asian parents join us by taking on various roles in the API or PTA events. When you step up, your child will follow. When you become a leader, your child will feel strong about their ability to contribute. When you become more visible and vocal, your child will take an active role in the school and community.

Be the hero you want to see first, then your child will follow.

Exercises

1. Ask your child to teach you something they love (a new app, a game, a skill, or even a TikTok trend!).

2. Choose one community activity to engage in with your child (e.g., a local club, volunteering, a sports team, or a church group).

3. For one week, speak only positive affirmations to your child, either out loud or in a journal.

Conclusion

In this book, I've shared many stories, including the misunderstandings and tensions that often arise between immigrant parents and their children. My hope is that these stories will illuminate the gap between both sides, revealing that—deep down—we all want to love and be loved.

All parents love their children and want the best for them. Likewise, children yearn for their parents' love and approval. However, cultural differences, generational shifts, and immigrant mindsets contribute to familial conflicts.

While values like hard work, academic excellence, and goal-driven ambition are strengths, they also come with challenges—insecurity, high expectations, and an authoritarian approach to parenting.

To help parents navigate these struggles while raising cross-cultural children, I've introduced seven key principles to foster growth for both parents and children.

Seven principles for raising cross-cultural children:

1. Master the art of communication

Communication is the foundation of any strong relationship. Don't slam the door—open it.

Practice active listening, remain calm, and guide with wisdom rather than reacting emotionally.

Give children praise and blessings, not just corrections.

2. Redefine success

Success is not just grades and achievements—it starts with health, emotional well-being, and strong relationships.

3. Let your children be themselves

Give them the space to grow, make mistakes, and become independent.

Your role is not to control their path, but to support their journey.

4. Model independence instead of preaching it

Children learn best by example, not lectures. Show them what independence looks like in:
- Emotional intelligence
- Health and well-being

- Self-image and confidence
- Building relationships

5. Help mend the fence before it breaks

When tensions rise, focus on repair.

Mental health is a critical concern. Parents need to be aware, be present, and be supportive.

6. Fill your own cup first

A parent who is emotionally and mentally fulfilled can offer genuine love, patience, and support to their children. Self-care is not selfish—it's essential.

7. Be the hero you want your child to See

The best way to raise resilient, kind, and successful children is to embody those qualities yourself.

When parents lament that today's children are not as "good" as they were in their own childhood, they often compare an idealized version of their younger selves to their children today.

They forget the struggles, mistakes, and mischief they had when they were young. Also, they do not realize that they have decades of life experience shaping their current perspective, while their children are still learning and growing. Rather than blaming children for not measuring up, parents should instead reflect on their own role in creating an environment where children can thrive.

Children, like flowers, need the right balance of nutrients, water, and sunlight to bloom. Not all flowers bloom at the same time. Some take longer, and that's okay.

Children are not parental property. They are their own masters that are responsible for shaping their own future. Parents are guides, coaches, and teachers, but ultimately, the journey belongs to the child.

The goal of parenting is not to control, but to empower. When we focus on nurturing, guiding, and leading by example, we allow our children to flourish in their own timing in their own way.

Acknowledgments

"Love is patient; love is kind." My dad and mom were my first teachers in parenting, and they often reminded me of this verse whenever I struggled with my children. When I had a big fight at home, they never criticized me or my children. Instead, they gently encouraged me to love unconditionally. They believed in us when I doubted myself. I cannot thank them enough for shaping who I am today as a mother, a coach, an author, and now, a publisher.

On my journey to learning patience, the most important companion has been my husband. He carried the responsibilities of raising our children, endured my temperament, and wiped away my tears on the darkest nights. Without his steady support, I could not have become the mother I am today.

To my children—I thank you for your naughtiness, your patience, and your love. Because of your rebellion, I learned to confront my own need for control. Because of your patience, I grew more loving, empathetic, and wise. Because of your love, my life is full of sunshine. You have been my greatest teachers, showing me how to use digital gadgets, introducing me to the arts, recommending books, and encouraging me to write my stories for other parents. Somewhere along the way, we became best friends.

My deep gratitude goes to my editor, Dr. Frances A. Chiu, who spent countless hours reading and revising my manuscript. Her wisdom helped me bring these stories to life. She not only refined my words, but also guided me to look deeper into my soul and expand my research. I am also sincerely thankful to Javier Prieto, my talented graphic designer, and to my meticulous copy editors, Jenelle Soo and Ethan Chau. Their care, creativity, and attention to detail ensured that this book reached its highest quality.

I also want to thank many friends who read my drafts and offered encouragement. Your feedback gave me courage and pushed me to keep going.

And finally, to my early supporters who preordered the book before it was even finished. Thank you for trusting me. Your generosity and faith touched me deeply and reminded me that this book was never my journey alone, but ours together.

Andy Chen

Benjamin Chan

Diane Erbeznik

Emily Fong Mitchell

Emmelyn Kim

Ivy Shen

Jamie Fossen

Jennifer Chiou

Jenny Liang

Jerry Xu

John Li

John Wu

Junping Gong
Karen S. Gee
Lijun Wang
Lilian Sun
Linda Qian
Lydia Flocchini
Manjit Basi
Michelle Kong
Michelle Pecak
Mike Nie
Min Ding
Min (Fennie) Feng
Mochen Ding
Nancy Zhang

Nyrka Riskin
Saba Syed
Shen Li
Sherry Hsi
Vernon D. Stewart
Wei Zhang
Yan Qi
Xiangchun Meng
Xiange Zheng
Xiaoping Liu
Xinghong Zhang
Yang Huang
Zhongkun Liu
Zhouyan Chen

Some of my supporters shared heartfelt insights on parenting, while others sent words of encouragement that kept me going throughout the writing journey.

- "You will help many parents. Keep shining!"

- "We are all just trying to be good moms while continuing to be good adults."

- "Can't wait to read your book!"

- "從造物主支取的母愛，用之不竭。" *(A mother's love, drawn from the Creator, never runs dry.)*

- "Don't be afraid to ask for help. Make time for yourself; find ways to bring joy into your life by focusing your emotional efforts on people and things that really matter.."

- "Congratulations! Wishing you all the success this book deserves."

- "Watching your child grow into who they're meant to be is priceless."

- "Share emotions as they arise - vulnerability heals generations."

- It's never easy and not always immediately rewarding, but watching your child grow into the adult they're meant to be is priceless

- "Crying keeps the mind and heart in balance."

- "Excited for Lucy and her powerful story."

- "Parenting is a difficult journey. Be kind to yourself and lead with love."

- "Give children space to grow and learn."

- "Lead by example."

- "Raising a child is like chess—one move can change everything."

- "Hang in there!"

- "Great job."

- "Looking forward to reading it."

- "Mom is the 定海神针—the anchor of the family."

- "Patience is one of the best parenting skills."

- "You rock, Lucy! Can't wait to read your new book."

More praises have been received from my network:

"Lucy beautifully normalizes the holistic, emotional, imperfect journey of parenting by sharing her own vulnerable stories and practical wisdom. She encourages parents to embrace both their blessings and lessons—her "blessons.", showing how shifting to a healthier mindset, seeking support, and letting go of perfection creates deeper connection, resilience, and joy for both parent and child." - **Michelle Pecak**, Founder of MY VIBE & CEO of Simple Smart Consulting

"This book is a must-read for every parent who wants to raise independent and resilient children today. Lucy Chen guides us through the challenges of parenthood, inviting us to defy limiting beliefs and a scarcity mindset and adopt a new approach towards happier and more fulfilled families." - **Mirna Eusebio Lithgow**, Award Winning & Best-Selling Author of *Leap Out Of Your Lane: The Playbook for Unlocking Your Success by Embracing Change.*

"Lucy Chen's *Good Moms DO Cry* is a book that understands you. It encourages you to feel those feelings as a parent. The highs and lows, but most importantly, finding the joy in the journey. In today's rapidly changing times, while navigating the playbook from first-generation immigrants, Chen gives you a framework so you can raise resilient children who can cry and rise." - **Marnie Maton**, CMO, CHOICE Healthcare Services, Best-selling Author of *Vote For You: Take Your Seat at the Table*

"*Good Moms DO Cry* is a must-read for parents that are looking for relatable stories and practical tips to raise their children, while navigating cultural traditions in our contemporary world. I highly recommend it!" - **Nyrka Riskin**, Speaker, Coach, and Author of *Unstoppable: How to Spice up your Brand, Create Opportunities, and Reach your goals.*

Appendix

Introduction

Chua, Amy. *Battle Hymn of the Tiger Mother*. New York: Penguin Press, 2011.

Lickona, Thomas. 2020. "4 Parenting Styles: How They Relate to a Child's Character." *Psychology Today*. June 2020. https://www.psychologytoday.com/us/blog/raising-kind-kids/202006/4-parenting-styles-how-they-relate-childs-character.

Chapter 1: Lose-Lose

Ali, Shahmir H, et al. 2022. "Family Involvement in Asian American Health Interventions: A Scoping Review and Conceptual Model." National Library of Medicine. December 2022.
https://pmc.ncbi.nlm.nih.gov/articles/PMC10576478/.

Besana, Tiffany, et al. 2020. "Asian American Media Representation: A Film Analysis and Implications for Identity Development." Taylor & Francis Online. April 2020.
https://www.tandfonline.com/doi/abs/10.1080/15427609.2020.1711680 .

Drubner, Stacey J. 2024. "Teens and Young Adults are at High-risk for Online Scams." Mass General Brigham EAP. January 2024. https://eap.partners.org/news_posts/young-people-at-high-risk-for-online-scams/.

Landsford, Jennifer. 2025. "Parents and Peers". Northern Virginia Community College. November 2025. https://pressbooks.nvcc.edu/psy236adolescentpsych/chapter/parents-and-peers/.

National Institute of Mental Health. 2025. "The Teen Brain: 7 Things to Know." November 2025. National Institute of Mental Health. https://www.nimh.nih.gov/health/publications/the-teen-brain-7-things-to-know.

NDTV News Desk. 2024. "Arizona Toddler Dies After Father Leaves Her In Hot Car For Hours." NDTV World. July 2024. https://www.ndtv.com/world-news/arizona-toddler-dies-after-father-leaves-her-in-hot-car-for-hours-6131904.

Premier Health. 2023. "Screen Addiction Affects Physical and Mental Health." Premier Health. May 2023. https://www.premierhealth.com/your-health/articles/health-topics/screen-addiction-affects-physical-and-mental-health.

Sedona Sky Academy. 2024. "Celebrity Worship Syndrome and Its Impact on Teen." Sedona Sky Academy. May 2024. https://www.sedonasky.org/blog/celebrity-worship-syndrome.

Zablotsky, Benjamin, et al. 2024. "Daily Screen Time Among Teenagers: United States, July 2021–December 2023." National Center for Health Statistics. October 2024. https://www.cdc.gov/nchs/products/databriefs/db513.htm.

Chapter 2: Bear Child in Parents' Eyes
Levin, Sydney. 2016. "Dad moves daughter's belongings to driveway to teach a lesson." AOL. July 2016. https://www.aol.com/news/2014-04-02-dad-moves-daughter-s-belongings-to-driveway-to-teach-a-lesson-20861695.html.

Chapter 3: Tiger Mother from Bear Child's Perspective
Delvecchio, Elisa, et al. 2020. "Parenting Styles and Child's Well-Being: The Mediating Role of the Perceived Parental Stress." National Library of Medicine. August 2020. https://pmc.ncbi.nlm.nih.gov/articles/PMC7909500.

Huynh, Lia. 2025. "The Hidden Struggles Inside the Asian Family: A Therapist's Perspective". liahuynh.com. November 2025. https://liahuynh.com/dysfunctional-asian-family-dynamics-asian-therapist-explains/.

Chapter 4: Principle 1: Communicate, Communicate, Communicate

Covey, Stephen R. *The 7 Habits of Highly Effective People.* New York: Free Press, 1989.

Dweck, Carol S. *Mindset: The New Psychology of Success.* New York: Ballantine Books, 2007.

Yoder, Megan. 2019. "Woman saves years of sticky notes from stepdad, brings him to tears with gift". WCNC. June 2019. https://www.wcnc.com/article/news/my-biggest-supporter-girl-saves-years-of-sticky-notes-from-stepdad-makes-emotional-gift/507-ff493114-bf6e-4072-bf25-db8199f569af.

Chapter 5: Principle 2: Success Redefined

Alvarez, Janet. 2019. "Immigrants outperform native-born Americans on two key measures of financial success." NBC News. June 2019. https://www.nbcnews.com/news/latino/immigrants-outperform-native-born-americans-two-key-measures-financial-success-n1020291.

Chen, Ava. 2024. "Princeton college consultants must prioritize accessibility and pedagogy, not profit." Command Education. September 2024. https://www.commandeducation.com/press/princeton-college-consultants-must-prioritize-accessibility-and-pedagogy-not-profit/.

Cooper, Preston. 2023. "New Study Investigates Why Elite Colleges Favor Rich Kids." *Forbes.* August 2023. https://www.forbes.com/sites/prestoncooper2/2023/08/22/new-study-investigates-why-elite-colleges-favor-rich-kids/.

Grossman, Joshua, et al. 2024. "The disparate impacts of college admissions policies on Asian American applicants." Nature. February 2024. https://www.nature.com/articles/s41598-024-55119-0.

Horowitch, Rose. 2025. "The Computer-Science Bubble Is Bursting." June 2025. https://www.theatlantic.com/economy/archive/2025/06/computer-science-bubble-ai/683242/.

Liu, Simu. *We Were Dreamers: An Immigrant Superhero Origin Story.* New York: William Morrow (HarperCollins), 2023.

National Centers for Environmental Information. 2025. "Significant Earthquake Information." NOAA. November 2025. https://www.ngdc.noaa.gov/hazel/view/hazards/earthquake/event-more-info/7843

Reyes, Miles, Ivy Song, and Apurva Bhatt. 2024. "Breaking the Silence: An Epidemiological Report on Asian American and Pacific Islander Youth Mental Health and Suicide (1999–2021)." The Association for Child and

Adolescent Mental Health. March 2024.
https://acamh.onlinelibrary.wiley.com/doi/10.1111/camh.1
2708.

Shin, Rachel. 2023. "A professor has tracked the colleges
of Fortune 500 CEOs for 20 years. He was stunned to
learn Ivy Leagues don't matter that much." *Fortune.* June
2023.
https://fortune.com/2023/06/14/fortune-500-ceo-colleges-
ivy-league/.

Verlenden, Jorge V., et al. 2024. "Mental Health and
Suicide Risk Among High School Students and Protective
Factors — Youth Risk Behavior Survey, United States,
2023." CDC. October 2024.
https://www.cdc.gov/mmwr/volumes/73/su/su7304a9.htm.

Chapter 6: Principle 3: Let Them ~~Fail~~ Fly

Lu, Dave. 2023. "How the Immigrant Scarcity Mindset
Holds Us Back." Hyphen Nation. November 2023.
https://www.davelu.com/p/how-the-immigrant-scarcity-
mindset.

Chapter 7: Principle 4: Show, ~~But Not~~ And Tell

Ancient & Oriental. 2025. "The Importance of the Fat
Lady in Chinese Tang Art". Ancient & Oriental.
https://www.antiquities.co.uk/collections/the-importance-
of-the-fat-lady-in-chinese-tang-art/ .

Bureau of Labor Statistics News Release. 2025.
"EMPLOYMENT CHARACTERISTICS OF FAMILIES —

2024." U.S. Department of Labor. April 2025.
https://www.bls.gov/news.release/pdf/famee.pdf.

Carney, Dana R., et. al. 2010. "Power Posing: Brief Nonverbal Displays Affect Neuroendocrine Levels and Risk Tolerance" *Sage Journals*. September 2010. https://journals.sagepub.com/doi/10.1177/0956797610383437

Fioravanti, Giulia, et al. 2022. "How the Exposure to Beauty Ideals on Social Networking Sites Influences Body Image: A Systematic Review of Experimental Studies." Springer Nature Link. January 2022. https://link.springer.com/article/10.1007/s40894-022-00179-4.

Robbins, Tony. 2025. "Identity and authenticity are the keys to unstoppable leadership". TonyRobbins.com. November 2025. https://www.tonyrobbins.com/blog/identity-and-authenticity-are-the-keys-to-unstoppable-leadership.

USAFacts team. 2023. "How many moms are in the labor force?" USAFacts. December 2023. https://usafacts.org/articles/how-many-mothers-are-in-the-labor-force.

Chapter 8: Principle 5: Mend the Fence
Baral, Swayam Prava, Parul Prasad, and Gyanendra Raghuvamshi. 2022. "Mental Health Awareness And

Generation Gap." National Library of Medicine. March 2022. https://pmc.ncbi.nlm.nih.gov/articles/PMC9129327.

McPhillips, Deidre. 2022. "90% of US adults say the United States is experiencing a mental health crisis, CNN/KFF poll finds." *CNN health.* October 2022. https://www.cnn.com/2022/10/05/health/cnn-kff-mental-health-poll-wellness/index.html.

Nishi, Koko. 2012. "Mental Health Among Asian-Americans." *American Psychological Association.* 2012. https://www.apa.org/pi/oema/resources/ethnicity-health/asian-american/article-mental-health .

Ring, David. 2021. "Mental and Social Health Are Inseparable from Physical Health". National Library of Medicine. June 2021. https://pubmed.ncbi.nlm.nih.gov/33877056/ .

Robertson, Karen. 2023. "Teacher Shares how he Helps Kids Beyond the Classroom – and Earns Extra Income – as a Life Coach for Kids – "…It's just the best!" Adventures in Wisdom. December 2023. https://adventuresinwisdom.com/how-teacher-helps-kids-beyond-the-classroom.

Chapter 9: Principle 6: Fill Your Cup First
McGlothern, Jenny. *Mama Needs a Refill.* Manuscripts LLC, Washington DC, 2023.

Smith, Angela M. *Stepping Into Love: a journey to self-healing.* Auckland: True Potential, 2023.

Varela, Natalia Vega, and Leyly Moridi. 2024. "The Free-Time Gender Gap: How Unpaid Care and Household Labor Reinforces Women's Inequality," Gender Equity Policy Institute. October 2024. https://thegepi.org/the-free-time-gender-gap.

About the Author

Lucy Chen is a leadership and resilience coach, speaker, and author whose work bridges professional leadership and family life. Born and raised in China, she arrived in the United States for graduate school in 1994. After earning an M.S. in Environmental Engineering from UCLA in 1996, she built a career across engineering, consulting, healthcare, and finance, prior to becoming a financial risk executive.

Lucy is a certified Human Potential Coach and Psychological Fitness Specialist and the founder of Gifted Coaching with over two decades of mentoring and coaching experience. More recently, she launched Gifted Books, a multi-language independent publishing house dedicated to helping diverse voices turn lived experience into meaningful books. A Distinguished Toastmaster, Lucy is known for her work in public speaking, career development, well-being, and resilience. She is a founding member of the San Francisco Chapter of Chief, a private network for women executives.

Good Moms DO Cry grew out of the intersection of Lucy's professional leadership experience and her personal journey as an immigrant parent. She believes that parenting—like leadership—is not about perfection or control, but about communication, trust, and repair. Lucy is also the author of *Build Resilience: Live, Learn, and*

Lead, a multi-award-winning book on resilience and leadership.

To learn more, visit:
www.GiftedCoaching.info
www.IAmLucyChen.com

To connect with her, visit:
www.linkedin.com/in/lucy-chen-ucla

www.ingramcontent.com/pod-product-compliance
Lightning Source LLC
Chambersburg PA
CBHW071309140726
47996CB00005B/1701